Nerves Out Loud

Critical Moments in the Lives of Seven Teen Girls

Edited by Susan Musgrave

ANNICK PRESS

TORONTO ✦ NEW YORK ✦ VANCOUVER

Annick Press Ltd.

We acknowledge the support of the Canada Council for the Arts, the Ontario Arts Council, and the Government of Canada through the Book Publishing Industry Development Program (BPIDP) for our publishing activities.

Edited by Barbara Pulling
Copy-edited by Elizabeth McLean
Designed by Irvin Cheung / iCheung Design
Cover image by T. Mischke / First Light

Cataloguing in Publication Data

Main entry under title:
Nerves out loud : critical moments in the lives of seven teen girls

ISBN 1-55037-693-4 (bound)   ISBN 1-55037-692-6 (pbk.)

1. Life change events. 2. Teenage girls. 3. Women authors, Canadian (English). - 20th century - Biography.* I. Musgrave, Susan, 1951-   .

HQ798.N47 2001   305.235   C2001-930208-8

The text was typeset in Franklin Gothic, Sabon, and Trixie.

Printed and bound in Canada

Distributed in Canada by
Firefly Books Ltd.
3680 Victoria Park Avenue
Willowdale, ON
M2H 3K1

visit us at www.annickpress.com

Distributed in the U.S.A. by
Firefly Books (U.S.) Inc.
P.O. Box 1338
Ellicott Station
Buffalo, NY 14205

Published in the U.S.A. by
Annick Press (U.S.) Ltd.

Introduction

In the film *Sliding Doors,* a young woman just fired from her job gets a chance to live two lives. One life begins as she races to catch a subway train in London and the doors close in her face, the other when she squeezes in through the sliding doors and rides home to find her boyfriend in another lover's arms.

Most of us never get to know how our lives might have turned out if things had gone differently. Instead, something big happens—and all of a sudden, your world is no longer the same. You can't go back to being what you were before this big thing occurred. And now you're on tenterhooks about what the future might hold.

In this book, seven writers look at the pivotal moments in their teenage years—an event or series of events that forever changed their lives. There will be something for every reader to identify with in these gutsy and straight-from-the-heart stories. Perhaps you're involved in championship sports, and you're thinking of calling it quits. Maybe you've started to experiment with drugs or alcohol. You might have lost a close friend, or a parent. You could have problems at home, might have experienced sexual or physical abuse. Or maybe you feel like a freak because you want to kiss your best friend, who is a girl. I hope in this book you'll find that whatever it is you're going through, you are not alone. "I am losing control and I am terrified," writes Karen Rivers, who, in her teen years, suffered from an eating disorder. She echoes our darkest fears: "I think: If people knew I did this, they would hate me."

No matter what fate doles out to you—whether the sliding doors slam shut in your face, or you ride the subway train home— there is hope, and so much possibility at the end of the tunnel. By fearlessly telling their stories, these writers give us all permission to speak out about our lives, our own terrible and beautiful teen-age years.

—Susan Musgrave

After the Flood

Melanie Little

You're supposed to be able to pin down the exact moment when things changed, right? Especially when things go wrong. You're supposed to be able to say: Up until then, everything was going okay. Everything was going just fine. And then—wham. *It* happened. The rest is history. Right?

Possible *It* moment #1: Summer, 1985.
My dad's car, or at least the one the people he works for let him drive. I've been babbling, giving him some big rationalization as to why I should maybe consider taking a break from figure skating, the only thing that has given shape to my life, tied each month and each year to the one before it. Dad says, "You're not a quitter, are you, Melanie?"

You have to get the tone right on this one. He doesn't say it as a challenge, the way some parents might—you know, in order to get you mad, to make you want to prove them wrong. He says it, instead, as if he's talking to himself. As if the possibility has dawned on him for the first time, and it's something he does not even want to consider, like the existence of aliens or of my love life. His daughter, the girl with the straight-A average and the skating medals holding up her bedroom walls, a quitter. It's said in the tone of Scully in *The X-Files*: "You don't actually believe in this horse-shit, do you, Mulder?"

Possible *It* moment #2: Summer, 1986.
(Have I mentioned I hate summer?) My workplace—only work was finished hours ago. A guy hovers above me like someone in a dream whose presence you can't for the life of you figure out. He's pudgy, but he's smiling, confident, wears his pudge like a trophy. He's vaguely familiar—I think he's friends with someone who works here. He comes closer and then his face changes. "Forget it, man," he says, to someone else who is there, though I can't see him. "I can't do it. She's had enough."

She's had enough. Enough of what? He could be talking about anything, for all I know of what's going on. Enough chocolate, enough wine, enough philosophical uncertainty. But suddenly, with the cold slap of sobriety, I know it is none of these. He gives a half-apologetic shrug, more to his friend than to me. It's this gesture, its measliness, that I will remember.

If I could plot these two points on a graph and find the point of intersection, I might have what we're looking for, the perfect pivot. If I could find it, that tip of the iceberg, could I return to it, scale it, even slide back down the other side?

Before: Skater

I make a list of the things I've quit:

Ballet

Tap

Jazz

Brownies

Baton twirling

Swimming lessons

Electric organ lessons

A novel I was writing, about running away

Gymnastics

Yearbook committee (they never let me have the camera)

Okay, so that's a lot. But there are two things I've always figured I'll never quit: school and skating. School because I'm pretty sure it would be illegal. Skating because I can't, it's not possible, my parents have invested everything in it, *I've* invested everything in it, I've had skate leather molded to my feet since I was five. Quitting is unthinkable.

I was already in love with figure skating by the time my grade two Religion teacher tried to teach us about Noah and the Flood. All I could think of as she spoke were the floods at the end of my skating sessions, when the Zamboni came on to clean the ice and we had to scamper off. The floods were necessary, of course, almost as necessary as the ice itself. They smoothed things out, covered the ruts, levelled the surface. They were written up on our daily schedules, neatly dividing one session from another, one level of skater from the next. But most of all, a flood meant the end of the skate. So it made perfect sense to me that a flood should be the chosen sign for the end of the world.

When you fall out of favor in skating, when your star dips down, you spend a lot of time hanging around the boards, trying to disappear. Maybe if you stay on the periphery like that, away from center stage, people will finally stop watching every little thing you do. Because the stands are always sprinkled with them, even at eight o'clock in the morning: people who watch. Mothers, coaches, judges doing research for upcoming test days and competitions, other skaters, even kids who've never been on skates in their lives. When you're out there on the ice you are fair game for all sorts of judgments, criticisms, predictions, speculations, rumors. (For example, the grade ten guys from my school have been hanging around the glassed-in lobby lately, taking bets on which one of us will lose her virginity next . . . to one of them, of course. Yeah, right.) It's like being on TV, only the people in the audience aren't faceless strangers. They're people you'll have to face tomorrow and tomorrow and tomorrow.

The rink's DJ plays "Relax" by Frankie Goes to Hollywood, a song that usually gets me pumped, sharpens my focus. But today I'm off-kilter and wobbly. My blades refuse to cut into the ice. Nothing's been going right all summer. The only time I can land my hardest jumps is at night, in my dreams. With the correspondence course I'm doing on top of everything else, I get six hours of sleep per night, max. Thanks to the dreams, I'm spending those six hours on the ice too.

The last two years of high school will be the hardest, I know, but I'm also heading into my biggest season for skating competitions ever—*if* I qualify. Getting extra credits now will free up another hour for training come fall. The correspondence course is The History of Ancient Civilizations. I've tried to figure out which civilization skating is most like, and I've come up with three possibilities: 1) The Roman Empire; 2) Medieval England; or 3) Ancient Crete. Rome, because we're like gladiators, fighting each other for gold medallions and for the praise of our emperor, the coach. Our blades are our swords and our bodies are our shields. Medieval England, because the practice time, and even the ice itself, is divided up into sections, like the feudal system. When you move up in the ranks, you get a sliver of fame, a better plot of land, and nicer armor. Ancient Crete, because of the Minotaur. I don't know exactly why I connect the Minotaur with skating. The Minotaur could be my coach, I guess, or even the judges, but it's more like something inside me, inside us. The huge, horned fear that lives down deep in the braiding of our intestines, rumbling to come out.

Usually summer is a respite from the double-lives thing: skating on the one foot, school on the other. In summer, you get more training done, and even though you're skating eight or nine hours a day, you can relax in your skin. You don't have to try to pass for normal with your teachers and the people in your classes. But this summer is different. It's like a damn aquarium in here, glass windows everywhere, people always gaping. Even worse than school. I've just turned fifteen. Recently, in the ultra-romantic environment of my parents' garage, I had my first kiss. His name was Bryant, and it started with a snowball fight. I zinged him in the head and then he grabbed me and held me down, snow-packed hand hovering above my face, legs and pelvis pushing into mine. After that, he took to kissing me at unpredictable times in semi-private places until the Friday night he dumped me for Natalie, who has bigger boobs as well as a flawless double axel. The snowball-fight snow was only fake snow, of course, summer-snow, leftover droppings from the Zamboni yard. Maybe that was the problem. Maybe true love requires real snow.

The previous Wednesday, a car had swung into the garage just as Bryant was reaching under my bra. The car was driven by Suzanne, the skating club's special spin coach. (A fifteen-minute lesson with Suzanne is like six solid hours on the Tilt-A-Whirl.) She was probably coming to badger my parents for the money they owe her, money everybody knows my parents don't have. Suzanne's cheap by comparison to the rest of them, but she's still around seventy dollars an hour.

When the adults at the arena catch wind of this little saga, they act as if it's the funniest thing they've heard all month. Maybe telling everyone about Bryant and me and the bra was Suzanne's way of getting revenge on my parents. Whatever the reason, the effect is unanimous: I am a laughingstock. Natalie and Bryant skate onto figure practice holding hands now, always taking two patches beside each other on the ice. It's hard to stop my foot from lurching in its tracing every time she giggles, which is often. Our coach tries to use what he sees as an exciting new rivalry to get us all to work harder, and he schedules group lessons for the three of us. These lessons do not go well, for me. The take-offs on my jumps are wild, and I keep opening up in the middle of the rotation so that I come down with arms and legs flailing, as if I'm a shot goose. The slouchers at the boards start skating away as soon as I approach.

I have what I'm sure is my last good day on the ice. You can always tell when something is going to come to an end, even if you don't want it to. It's like that with guys and close friends, and it's like that with things you're good at, too.

On this last good day I go through my free-skate program, the one to the music from *Fiddler on the Roof*. It's the first time in weeks that I make it all the way through without stopping or falling. Brian Orser, world champion, is watching from the boards. After practice he walks by me and says, "I love your program." He uses the present tense, "love," as if this program is something that will be skated in future competitions, maybe the Nationals, Worlds, even the Olympics. As if it's an accessory that I have, like a favorite earring. At this moment, still, I could have that future.

But instead, I go to the dressing room and take off my skates and watch the steam rise from my stockinged feet. I take off my dress and my leg warmers and my tights right there on the bench. I have always, always, waited until I got home to change out of my skating clothes. The arena is only four minutes away by bike, so why bother changing in the dank, too-loud, too-public dressing room? My street clothes stay balled up in my skate bag, usually, like an identity I'm reluctant to get back to. But today, the last good day, I ride home in shorts and a tank top.

During: Quitter

Annabel, my only nonskater friend, calls me to come over. She's taking two weeks off work because she's had a nose job and it has to heal. She doesn't look much different to me. Her nose is still big, and she's still beautiful. Clearly, though, she's thrilled. I've never known her to wear makeup, but now her face is coated with it. It makes her look unreal, as if her features are floating in front of her face. "It's to cover the bruising, you know, on the nose," she says, because I must be staring. But she even has makeup on her chin.

Annabel has called me over for a purpose. She wants to talk about sex.

Sex is this occult thing for me. So it terrifies me that Annabel, whose ambition is to be a librarian, is taking it into her life, moving over to make room for it with incredible calm. Her summer job is at a center for men with mental disabilities—which, as it turns out, is a hotbed of teenaged sexual activity. When she and her coworkers aren't wiping noses or cleaning up shit sculptures, they're huddled behind doors in unused lounges perfecting the art of the blow job. At first I think she means on the male inmates, but I'm pretty shocked even when she assures me that the staff members only do it on each other. Annabel hasn't had much experience at shocking people, and she's loving this. She whips out a beer bottle to demonstrate how it's done. All I can think about is that the beer bottle is empty, and that I want to get the hell out of her room.

During the past school year, Annabel and I were drinking buddies. We didn't do it often, only for school dances, and since there are only three high schools in town, it worked out to about twice a month. The rest of the time, we didn't drink a thing. But those Friday nights, we were blitzkrieged, bombed, obliterated— all those words used to describe wars and hockey games.

We live in a small town, and neither of us has siblings. That put everything Annabel and I did under a microscope, so we were forced to develop a whole underground world of places to drink. We'd usually start off at a restaurant, where we'd pour vodka into half-emptied bottles of O.J. in the washroom. The vodka was stored in contact lens–solution containers to head off the cops.

Our half-eaten hamburgers paid for and our purses fully stocked, we'd hit our real destinations. The parking lot at Zellers. The bushes behind city hall. The amphitheater down by the water, where we watched the boats go by and tried to ignore the smell from the sewage plant beside us. Once, the garden of an old folks' home. Our mission was always the same: complete, personality-erasing hammerdom. This single, simple goal brought me great inner peace. I'd tried getting drunk with skaters only once and cried all the way through it. With the skaters I couldn't stop think-ing of my problems—my warring parents, our lack of money, the bitchy out-of-town skaters who boarded at our house and wrote mean things about me in their diaries. I thought about my flat chest, my sagging jumps, my constant headaches, my sinking suspicion that my coach didn't want to teach me any more. Drinking with Annabel was completely different. With her I could stare out at the lake, think about whatever came into my head, think about nothing at all, even. The results of our labors were not a matter of skill or training or timing or luck. There was no stress involved, except for the fear of being stopped. By the time we reached the bottom of the bottle, we would be victorious. We would cease to be ourselves.

"I admire you," people sometimes say to me now. "You worked your whole life to be one thing, a champion figure skater, and then you had the guts to stop when it wasn't working out. That took a lot of courage."

Horseshit, Mulder.

Weeks past my last good day, my back starts to hurt. It hurts the way it does when I'm starting my period, multiplied by a million. It feels as if someone is threading a gigantic needle from the bottom of my spine all the way up to my neck. Everything else—boys, parents, boarders, coaches—falls out of my mind. All that is real is this needle, and this thread. My vision is a wash of red: I can barely see the other skaters watching and judging. I start to land all my jumps, to center my spins. The pain is a compass helping me find my way. I tell people about the needle, but I'm skating too well for them to take it seriously. I don't care what Bryant and the others are up to. I do notice that many of the girls are doing a lot of crying, though. The summer is coming to an end, and people are preparing to go back to their home cities. Friendships will be interrupted, maybe lost. The boarders at my house stay up nights, packing; I can hear them through the wall. I sleep anyway, still pulled along by the thread. For once, I don't dream.

Test day comes, on the last day of summer school. I'm trying a figure test and a free test, both of which I'm hopelessly unready for. The test schedule is practically empty. Most of the other skaters did their tests back in July, arrived at this place already set to move up to the next level.

Somewhere between getting up on test-day morning and skating onto the ice, the thread breaks. The pain is all over me now, moving around inside like a swarm of snakes. I skate some horrible figures, my blades slashing at the brackets and turns. I fail the figure test. Then it's time for the free skate. As I sit on the bench visualizing the double axel I *have* to land, the final bits of red erupt from the top of my spine and shoot into my head, where they swim in front of my eyes as huge, blinding dots. I'm screaming from the intensity of the headache, and my voice bounces off the half-full stands like a distorted version of the "Yay Melanie" cheers of my fantasies. The red dots burst the surface, and suddenly they're all over my face, my chest, my arms. Now other people can see them, and they rush me to the doctor. I can't stop screaming.

My mother thinks I'm going to die, and the doctors suspect it, too. They give me a spinal tap, plunging a real needle deep into my lower back. They're expecting to find meningitis, because I'm a middle-class teenager and that's who's been getting it lately. But it's encephalitis instead. They describe it as an inflammation of the brain. It sounds like a nightmare that's morphed into a medical condition.

I'm in hospital for two weeks, in the isolation ward because I'm contagious. I'm hooked up to an IV and have to ask permission to go to the bathroom. Not one of the departing skaters calls to say good-bye or to ask how I am. My coach doesn't call, either.

I hear the doctor talking to my mother outside the door. "This thing is often triggered by extreme stress," he says. "Essentially, she's done this to herself."

I do not, in fact, quit. That *would* require guts. What I do is much easier. I simply never go back.

Still, the result is the same. The Unthinkable.

After: Melanie Who?

Summer again, one year later. Even though skating's kaput, this summer, like every summer that's gone before it, must be filled. There's no question of "doing nothing": my family's never heard of it. My mother has a new job as the supervisor of a kids' playground at a swanky resort on the lake, a crappy job that for some reason everyone seems to feel she is lucky to have. She gets the resort to hire me on as her helper.

The whole resort is staffed by high school kids who treat it as their own private club. Their parents, all of whom have tons of dough, sometimes appear on the shore, emerging from their huge boats like gods. Taking a break from their million-dollar cottages to visit with their friends, the resort's owners. At least that's the way my mother describes it to me, as we gear up for our bike rides home along the dirt road and then the highway. Of course we can't afford a second car. Skating is over, but we're still paying for it. I hear horrifying figures hissed between my parents when they think I'm asleep. Ten thousand, fifty thousand, a hundred thousand. Whatever they owe, I know we don't have it. Will probably never have it. My legs still ache at night, the same way they would after an eight-hour day on the ice. "Phantom pain," my mother says.

The resort is a bit like the arena, except on another planet altogether. Skaters tend to think they're special, shiny. Silver. But these people—these people are golden. At the top of the glittering mass is a pair of twins with permanent tans and voices that are always slightly husky, as if they're just getting over colds. The twins are beautiful, of course, and they do everything just well enough. Nice, normal things that get you the respect of boys, like windsurfing, building campfires, and flirting exactly the right amount with the paying guests. They don't only get invited to parties, the parties themselves are planned around their availability.

One thing about this summer is the same as all the skating-filled ones before it: it's me and my mother against the world. We have different roles to play now, and we actually enjoy the variety. There is a new barrage of at least fifty little kids every Monday. My mother has their fun strictly scheduled: thirty minutes for water play, fifteen for mud pies, twenty for kiddie aerobics, twenty for story-time, twenty for a nap, forty-five for arts and crafts. My job is to herd them from one activity to the next. The kids fascinate me. I love to watch the way their little cliques form, break up, and re-form, each time with minor shifts. The ones who are left out always have completely bewildered looks on their faces: What the hell just happened here?

I don't hang out with the other resort workers much because our schedules are so different. They seem to spend their days on an endless series of breaks between giving guests lessons on how to use the Sea-Doos. At first I try to infiltrate these break zones on my lunch hour, but it feels too much like crashing a party. I give up and eat my sandwich in the nursery with my mom and Gloria, the resort's sixty-year-old head babysitter. I'm busy, too, going to lunch-hour aerobics and sticking my finger down my throat over the toilet every time I eat. I'm careful to use the bathrooms reserved for guests so that none of the other "staffers" catches on. My mother says eating disorders are strictly for stupid people, and I agree. But the hard truth is that no one puts on the pounds like an athlete who stops training. When I looked in the mirror this spring the person I saw wasn't Melanie. It was someone else who'd swallowed Melanie, someone fatter but with invisible skin, because you could still see me inside her.

Even though I don't talk to them, I am aware, very aware, of the boys who work here, boys who light up the dining room and the beach and the tennis courts. These are, to my mind, wonderful boys: outgoing, good-looking, popular, classy. Invariably, they go to the high schools in the north and west ends of town, the ones that offer Latin and Drama. These are the boys I've glimpsed in the demented hazes of my Friday-night dance excursions with Annabel. Though such boys rarely stay at the dances for longer than a minute. They're much too cool for that.

In August, when I've shed about ten pounds, one of the most beautiful ones begins hanging around the playground towards closing time. It's embarrassing to have to walk around the yard, picking up toys, smoothing down the sandbox, with Gary standing there watching me, but it's good, too. My mother pretends not to notice him, but she starts making me tidy up the indoor playroom instead.

A week later Gary grabs my arm as I'm charging out of aerobics. I'm red-faced, sweating and stinking, but I guess he doesn't care. He grips my forearm, leaning forward so much as he talks that the lock of hair hanging over his left eye actually gets damp from my forehead. He shakes it out, laughing, flicking moisture back onto me. He tells me to come to the outdoor hot tub that night after work.

My mother will never let me go, I know, so I don't ask her. When she goes outside to start tidying, I run out the back door and all the way down to the rec center. Gary is in the tub with another guy, Jeff, but as soon as I get there Jeff takes off, smirking. I have my bathing suit on under my clothes, so I tear them off. I figure I can stay for about five minutes, dry off, get dressed, run back, and tell my mom I went to the bathroom. I sink into the scalding water, my heart pounding. I feel like a lobster being boiled. I hear laughter behind me, and when I finally work up the nerve to look at Gary he's getting out of the tub.

One of the beautiful twins is there, dressed properly for the suddenly cold evening in jeans and a jacket. Gary stands talking to her, not even acknowledging me. I feign great interest in the "Rules and Regulations" sign. After about ten minutes of this, Gary and the twin walk off together. I stay in the tub for a long time—not waiting for him, because I know he's not coming back, but simply unable to move. When I finally do climb out my skin is puckered and red. I go to the bathroom to throw up nothing, and then I go back to the playground. My mother's bike is gone.

Once, at the public library, I'd seen this book lying on a table. It had a really stupid title, *Why Don't I Fit In?* or something like that. I opened it to a random page, and it was saying you should consider your peer group not as a bunch of rivals but as a single sports team. *Your* team. I try to picture all the kids at the resort as some big basketball outfit, the Raptors, maybe, but I can't help remembering that the one time I played basketball in gym, all I could manage was a wild (and thankfully unsuccessful) throw at the wrong hoop.

The staff at the resort are gearing up for a big, all-night, end-of-summer party. I want to go to this shindig with an urgency I don't even begin to understand. No. I don't just want to go. I need to go.

I beg my mother, but I don't get anywhere. She thinks the resort kids are a bunch of spoiled, oversexed, degenerate partiers.

But she wants them to like her, too, and so I start bugging her about it in front of them. Please, please, please, I say. It's all right, Mrs. Little, they say. We'll take care of her. We'll make sure she's all right. You can trust us! Don't you think you can?

School is starting in a week: my final year. Last year, my first academic year without skating, passed in a haze of sameness. Six hours of classes a day, day in, day out. No missed days because of practices, no missed weeks because of out-of-town competitions. How did people stay sane doing that year after year? I wondered. I felt invisible, a ghost. My feet barely seemed to make contact with the floor when I walked down the halls. It was as if the skates were still on my feet.

This party at the resort seems to belong to the new school year, somehow: a kind of orientation. If I can go and fit in and have a good time, everything will be all right from then on. I'm convinced of it.

My mom lets me go. When we get on our bikes that morning, she asks me if I've remembered to pack my overnight things: toothbrush, contacts case, glasses, pyjamas (god, Mom), a change of clothes. She ties a sleeping bag to her pack, offering to set it up for me in the playroom after all the kids have gone home. Tomorrow is Saturday, the last day for the children's camp, and I'll have to get myself up and be ready for work. She slips some extra chocolate into my bag.

I drag myself through the workday, half-hoping it will never end. When it does, I procrastinate, take extra-long getting ready, even spread out the sleeping bag on the playroom floor myself. By the time I finally wander into the staff housing area, it feels as if the party is sputtering out. People are hunkered down in various trailers and cabins, talking about nothing much. I don't have any alcohol of my own and some people share with me. I learn to start demanding it as soon as I stumble onto a new gathering; it earns me both more booze and more respect. I spend most of the night like that, walking from place to place, telling people to give me drinks.

I end up gulping wine and watching the sun rise with Mark, a guy I can't stand who's the only person here from my own high school. I doze off on the dock, and when I wake up my contact lenses are suctioned to the curves of my eyes. I somehow find my bag, lurch into the first trailer I see and pull out the contacts, replacing them with my old pop-bottle specs. There's a heap of jackets in the corner, and I lie down on them. I start to drift off again, so I remove the glasses and let myself fall asleep.

When I come to, I don't know where I am. Not one god-damned clue. I feel the lump of my glasses trapped underneath me. Things without them are a blur at best. There's a pudgy guy back-ing away from me. I hear him say, "She's had enough." Then I guess I fall back asleep. But when I open my eyes again, far into the morning, the image of the pudgy guy is still there, right where I left it. Or where it left me.

The only other thing I remember that morning is what I've been dreaming. Usually, my dreams are semirealistic, confined mostly to double axels and other jumps that were never too far beyond my reach. But this time it was a triple axel, the hardest jump any female skater has ever landed. When I first woke up I was, for a brief moment, very happy.

It's past ten when I finally leave the trailer. My mother is corralling the kids into sides for Red Rover, but she stops when I drag myself into the playground. Everyone is quiet, staring, even the four-year-olds. My mother tells me to go to the washroom and clean myself up. I still haven't changed; my pyjamas and today's clothes languish in the bag I left in the trailer. I will never go back to pick that bag up.

I sit down on the toilet and find blood on the inside of my shorts. It hurts to pee. Oh my god. Where are my panties? My panties are gone.

When I get back to the playground my dad is there, waiting in his car. I get in and he drives me home. I reek of alcohol, and he, a nondrinker for ten years, breathes air out his nose in disgust. It is an ugly day.

At the supper table that night, no one talks. If things were normal I'd be feeling relief, because my mom is no longer, as of this afternoon, my boss. I try to concentrate on that, try to crack a smile, though god knows who I think I'm kidding. "Well, Mrs. Little," I say, looking at my mother, "I quit." Nobody laughs.

Not knowing what people think about you is one thing; not knowing what they know about you is another. And not knowing what there *is* to know about you—that's exactly like walking around in a nightmare. I figured out a long time ago that all I had to do to end a bad dream was to squeeze my eyes tight until I woke, but it's a trick that doesn't work when you're already awake.

Back at school, there is a part of me that's still alive, keeping up my average, applying to universities, even acting in a play. Continuing on a kind of path. Unbelievably (especially to me), I'm asked out by a nice boy with a one-syllable name and an after-school job delivering flowers for his family's business. I burn with shame, terrified that this boy might find out what I've done. Somehow an entire school full of people who've never set foot on resort property know all about the end-of-summer party and what I did there. They're not telling me, though. It's rumored I had sex with at least three guys; it's rumored there are pictures. People start singing "Girls on Film" when I come down the hall. The word *rape* is never used.

Annabel has a new friend, this Jean chick who actually wrinkles her nose when Annabel introduces us. I want to tell Annabel that this mess is all her fault, because of the beer bottle tutorial, but I know that's ridiculous. And anyway, Annabel doesn't really look at me. She stands beside Jean and floats.

I think a lot about those long-ago dances. Annabel and I would laugh for days afterwards about the ridiculous stuff we'd done when we were drunk, reconstructing the evening slowly, piecing it together stupid thing by stupid thing. Sometimes a month would go by and one of us would remember one thing more. What if the resort party turns out to be like that? What if I'm walking down the street some day, or working at my job, and Wham!—I remember it all? Or even a part of it?

That's what I'm afraid of, now.

After the first dance of the year I decide to ditch my nice-boyfriend date and walk home by myself. I walk very, very slowly. I stop a lot. By four a.m. I'm in the middle of the highway. It's the same highway whose traffic I can hear from my bedroom window, the one I always worry my cat will die on. I tread the dotted line in the center, pretending it's a tightrope. With holes in it. It wouldn't be strictly accurate to say that I want to die. But it wouldn't be strictly accurate to say that I want to live, either.

The end of my street comes into view, and pretty soon I can see the back of my house. I left my bedroom light blazing—I can see the wall behind my bed, still littered with medals and ribbons. It's four-thirty in the morning. Almost time for the figure skaters to start getting up.

Fourteen Turns

Carellin Brooks

1. The boyfriends.

I was walking across the grass in front of my high school when I saw them. It was one of those spring days when everything in the world seems to be made up of light. I had my eyes on the ground ahead of me, digging into the green. Then I looked up and froze.

Mike and Scotty, my two boyfriends, were coming towards me. And they were talking.

Actually, it wasn't strictly correct to call Mike and Scotty my two boyfriends. The fact was that the week before, I had cheated on Mike with Scotty, even if cheating at this stage in my life consisted of necking, not sex. Only I didn't have the sneaking-around part of cheating down very well, because I'd been necking with Scotty at the bus stop midway between my house and Mike's when Mike walked by. I jumped over the back of the bus bench, but it was too late. By the time I got home Mike was sitting on my front porch, smoking furiously. He sniffled ostentatiously and gazed at me with wounded eyes.

Inside, my family glared at me. "How could you do that to poor Mike?" my foster mother demanded. "Slut," said my foster brother, sotto voce.

So the last two people I expected to be coming my way, practically arm in arm, were Scotty and Mike. Especially because after the bus-stop incident, I'd sort of dumped Mike for Scotty, not that I put it that way to him. And if that wasn't enough to feel guilty about, I had snuck Scott into my room that same weekend so that we could sleep together (though not have sex).

This was possible because my room, in the large house my family rented near the university, was in the basement and had its own separate entrance. I'd bartered the subterranean quarters for the chance to decorate as I saw fit, and my white walls were spray-painted with DayGlo orange and green slogans, plus the ballpoint annotations of my friends. The room had a small window near the top of the wall and a closet without a door, and it was here that I had pushed Scotty, behind my dresses, when I'd heard the creak of my foster father's foot on the stairs early the following morning.

I don't know why I hadn't thought of it before, the possibility that Tom might pay one of his visits that Monday. The fact was, I tried to think about what happened between my foster father and me as little as possible. I lived in two worlds. There was the daytime one, where I hung out with my friends, skipped some of my classes, smoked a little pot, shoplifted recreationally, and got the A grades that enabled me to do those things without much official notice. Then there was the world between me and my foster father, the dark space that had opened up three years ago, when I was eleven. That was the summer Tom had taken me for a walk and asked to be the one to whom I lost my virginity.

Since then, he had tried persuasion. This took the form of description: Tom liked to tell me what it was he wanted to do, and how, and how much, and when. He asked, in other words, and I said no, not once but many times, in as many ways as I could. And then there were the visits at night, where he pleaded to be allowed to at least suck my nipples. I let him, most times, because I had refused him so much else so often. But mostly I lived above ground as much as possible, forgetting during the day that such things happened, that anyone wanted me in this way.

With Scotty in the closet (large-sized pointy shoes protruding, if I had dared to look, from under my New Wave thrift-shop crinolines) and Tom sitting on my bed, trying to touch me while I squirmed away ("No! Not now!" I kept hissing, but he saw nothing particular in that day's refusals), the two places I lived in had collided in the realm of the undeniable. I used the only survival skill I had. After I had finally got rid of Tom and managed to spirit Scotty out the back door while the family was upstairs eating breakfast, I did my best to carry on as if nothing had actually happened.

2. The schoolyard.

What were Mike and Scotty doing together, I wondered now? It was lunchtime. The bell would ring at any moment, gathering us from our scattered fast-food forays and funnelling us back into the hallways. What, I thought, remembering the scene Scotty must have heard that morning in my closet, had he said to Mike? I hadn't had time to talk to him after Tom left, just pushed him out the back door at the first opportunity. This was the first time I had seen him since. Would he have told Mike? And if he had, what would Mike think?

As they came closer, both of them started talking at me. I heard Mike first.

"That bastard," he said. And then, explaining, "Scott told me what happened."

I looked over at Scott. He met my gaze.

"Let's kill him," he said.

3. Things Tom did.

Nobody ever says this, but having a thirty-year-old man lusting after you when you are a teenager is not all bad. At least, I didn't think it was. Oh, there were enough icky things, all right:

Tom buying me contraceptive sponges at the pharmacy for our long-awaited (on his part, anyhow) loss-of-virginity date;

Tom telling me, when I woke up one afternoon in the living room, that he had touched me in my sleep, and that I had liked it;

Tom asking, asking, begging actually, while his wife was in the next room, while his son was upstairs, while the two of them stayed carefully elsewhere, seemingly innocent, seemingly unaware.

But a grown man, asking (again and again and again) for something I had, something only I could give him! I couldn't help but feel flattered, even as it sickened me, this sense that I possessed something barely guessed at that might make men like Tom, men who were bigger and older and more powerful, plead. And then there was the money. I had never lived in a house where there was so much food, so much in the way of allowance, such a cavalcade of boxes from the bakery. New glasses. Visits to the dentist. Store-bought clothes instead of the kind I'd had as a child, neighbors' hand-me-downs pulled wrinkled and smelling faintly of other peoples' homes from green garbage bags. In Tom's house we bought entire boxes of oranges and grapefruits just for making juice. Enormous cookers of soup simmered on the stove, and the fridge was endlessly and invisibly refilled, as in a fairy story. There was so much, all the time, that I almost forgot about the years when there hadn't been enough: food, clothes, money. Or room for me. There hadn't been Tom then, either, but the trade-off seemed clear. Not exactly fair, maybe, but at least I knew what I was getting.

4. Acid dates.

The first drug I ever tried was marijuana. By the time I came to Tom's, I was an old hand at pot; my biological parents were hippies who smoked it regularly and taught me to call the weed "incense" in company, so that I wouldn't give them away. I liked the smell of pot. It seemed comforting, homey and familiar. My parents hadn't cooked much.

Tom liked getting me high. A sort of wolfish look came over him when he was passing the joint. He would give pot to me, to my friends, to anyone, in fact, just so long as he could get me into that dreamy land that he must have thought would make me more receptive to his advances.

I came home from school one afternoon high on acid. My foster father stood on the front porch and watched, bemused, as I ran up the street in my socks. It had started to rain, heavy, fat drops that turned the pavement dark within seconds, and as I ran I watched the fabric saturate with wet, so that the socks flopped around my feet. I came back onto the porch. "What are you on?" he asked me with amused tolerance. This was a man who always offered the joint, who slipped me gin-and-lemons on hot days.

I said, "Nothing." The word echoed, and I started to laugh. I loved acid, loved how far away I was and yet how incredibly detailed everything became. It was a place where I understood everything, a place Tom couldn't touch me.

And he didn't. He turned and went back into the house, his hand waving me away in a gesture of disgust. I stayed on the porch, smiling to myself, watching the rain.

What else I tried:

Mushrooms.

Cookies infused with THC at parties.

Speed, in the form of far more than the manufacturer's recommended dose of diet pills. They didn't work, though. They only made me feel slow and heavy.

Gin mixed with powdered lemonade at afternoon matinees, not to mention any other kind of drink my friends and I could get our hands on: kegged beer brought in from the next state over, where it was stronger; bottles obliging strangers bought for us at the corner store.

But acid was the best. Going downtown for the afternoon—downtown was where we always went, the bad kids, the roamers, the ones who hung out instead of going directly home after school—looking in shop windows, seeing the mannequins move and then realizing it was actually the window hangers, arranging a new display. Wow.

5. Doctor No.

Despite the drugs, some petty shoplifting, and the not-sex with Scott, Mike, and other boys, I was not a particularly good delinquent. Some lunchtimes I snuck into the library, hoping nobody would see me, and spent the hour engrossed in words. My favorite recreational reading was cautionary. I loved books that purported to be the first-hand stories of girls who got pregnant by accident ("I just wanted somebody to love me"), kids who became hooked on drugs, teens living on the streets. There were no books about teens being harassed by family members for sex, though if there had been no doubt I would have read those too. I was ignorant in strange, shaming ways; when I first started to bleed, I was so unacquainted with the structure of my own parts that I had to ask my foster mother, with much embarrassment, how I could go to the bathroom with a tampon in.

Now it was two years later, I was fourteen, and my foster

mother was taking me to the doctor. We didn't talk much during the drive, although questions occur to me now, years later. My foster mother was British, with a steely, quiet accent, a middle parting in her straight brown hair. She was a modern dance student who dressed neatly and without much show, and who, when pushed, would stand in the doorway, stomp her foot, contort her face and say with controlled fury, "I—am—so—*angry!*"

My foster mother guided me into the doctor's office. We sat down, and in her steely voice she said, "I've brought her here for contraception."

The doctor was a man, kindly. I hadn't seen him before. He looked at me and then at her. To me he said, "Are you having sex?"

"No," I said.

"Are you planning on having sex?"

"No," I said. In fact, inasmuch as I was capable of planning, I was planning not to have sex, to avoid sex, to keep from having sex with the man who wanted to have sex with me. "No," I said, and he must have seen it in my eyes, how I implored him: *Don't make me. Don't give me to him.*

"Why don't you come back when she's ready to have sex," he suggested, gently, to my foster mother. She took me away, although she seemed reluctant. We didn't speak on the drive back, either.

Questions occur to me now. Questions like: Who told you to? Why did you think I needed it? Who did you think I was going to have sex with?

Why didn't you ask me?

Why didn't I ask you?

6. What we took.

My friend Liz—Olivia, she liked to be called, on a lark—was a good shoplifter, maybe the best among us. She drifted around the 7-11 next to our school, singing to herself and flinging big-ticket items—chocolate bars, baked goods, ice cream—into the cavernous depths of her black shoulder bag, while we, her more nervous friends, grouped ourselves near the three-for-a-dollar hot-dog cooker and eyed the oblivious counter boy. Smiling sunnily, Liz would come up to the cash and pay for a packet of gum or a Popsicle, splitting the extras with us in the yard later. For Liz, it never seemed to matter much what she stole, simply that she could do it.

Liz also stole clothes from the big department stores downtown, returning them later for cash with their tags still attached, claiming they didn't fit or she hadn't liked them. I kept a pair of tight capri Calvins she gave me for years after I stopped wearing them, just because I was impressed by her daring and the way she tossed it off.

Everyone else stole, too, most of us in pairs. One person covered the possible approaches, looking for salesclerks or detectives, while the other pocketed the things. We stole stuff that was of little account except to us: lipsticks, barrettes, costume jewelry, makeup. Once a bunch of us got taken downstairs for what the store cops called "theft of services": all drinking from the same bottomless coffee cup. We sneered and rolled our eyes. Try prosecuting us for twenty-five cents, we told them, like we were tough.

I was more scared than the others, so I did most of my stealing alone. That's how I got caught that spring, lifting a pair of purple plastic clip-on earrings in the garishly lit main corridor of a department store. I didn't see the man until he was at my elbow, hand on my arm. We went down to the small detectives' office, me silent with shock, him with satisfaction. He wrote up the form, told me they would prosecute, that they always prosecuted, that I would have a record. Then he asked for my parents' name and phone number.

I appealed to him not to call, because I suddenly saw what it would mean. But the man either ignored or refused to understand my terror. Maybe he thought he was teaching me a lesson. He called Tom; Tom was home. He came downtown and got me. "Well," he said when we got to the car, "you know what this means."

"What?" I said, though I knew, really, in the sick part of yourself that knows everything bad that can happen.

"You did the worst thing you could do," Tom said, "so now I'm going to do the worst thing I can do to you."

I knew he meant sex, that he was going to force himself on me, that my evasions were at an end. Tom's formulation wasn't particularly logical, but I understood it perfectly: I had been caught, now I was to be punished. That the punishment was the thing I dreaded most from him was not incidental. That it agreed with none of his professed precepts—sex, he always said, was going to be fun, I should try it, I would like it, he would make it good for me—did not seem to matter.

That afternoon the house filled with a slowly gathering dread, making it impossible for me to think or feel or act normally. I never acted normally with Tom and his family, anyhow. There were always the unspoken things behind the family life we affected to lead, the way Tom looked at me when he passed me a glass behind his wife's back, the thought that perhaps someone else knew or might at any moment guess. I called Liz finally, furtively, from my bedroom extension.

"I have to get away," I cried over the phone. "Something's happened."

Liz knew what I meant by "something." She knew all about Tom. We carried each others' burdens, kids my age: how someone threw up after meals, another girl's mother who drank in the morning, a friend's abortion, someone else who had started to take drugs every day, as a matter of course. We thought that we were strong enough for these details and, more importantly, that the adults in our lives weren't. We guarded each other. "Come over," she said.

In Liz's bedroom I paced and cried some more. "He's going to make me. He will, he will."

"What did he say?"

"He said he was going to do the worst thing ever to me, and that's what he means. I can't stay there, Liz, I can't let him do it."

Liz went out of the room for a minute, then came back to

take me to her father. I only ever saw him that once; I remember him as a small, ineffectual man, buttressed in a corduroy La-Z-Boy that seemed to swallow his frame. He turned from the television. "Liz says you want to stay here for a while."

I nodded.

"Why don't you want to go home?"

I shook my head, crying. "I can't tell you," I said. My secret was a weight no adult could possibly bear. *What he wanted from me; where he laid his hands.* Or was it that the adults were in it together, that they protected their own as we did ours, with a wall of silence? I wasn't sure. I just knew that I had nothing to say to him, as he had almost nothing to say to me.

"Well," he said after a pause, "I'm sorry, but I don't think you can stay here. Not if we don't know why it is you're leaving." He did not say this in any sort of vindictive way. He was not unkind. He knew there was something wrong, even if he did not want to think too much about what that something might be. The Man Who Did Not Want to Become Involved.

"I'm sorry," Liz said. She stood in the bedroom doorway, watching me put on my coat. I moved clumsily, because I was unsure where I was going next. We looked full on at each other, recognizing what neither of us could say. This was a world of adults. They did not understand, and they did not help you. We knew that, had in fact always known it. We knew we were on our own; it was only that sometimes we forgot.

7. Helplines.

I called the youth emergency line from a phone booth. Outside, darkness. I rifled the phone book with one hand as I listened to the far-off ring. Surely there were shelters for girls like me, teenagers who couldn't go home? I had no idea. Despite my lurid reading material and my imaginings—running away had always seemed tragically romantic and brave, something a more adventurous person would have no doubt done long ago—I had never left before. Then again, things had never been this bad.

The man who answered the phone sounded young. I told him I needed a place to stay.

"How old are you?" he asked me. He wanted to know when I had left, whether my parents had noticed that I was missing, if I had communicated with them in any way. When I said they were my foster parents, his tone sharpened. "You're in the care of the government?"

"Yes."

"I'm sorry," he told me. "You'll have to call your social worker. We can't help you."

I didn't argue. I simply hung up, desolate. *We can't help you.* It seemed more than a statement for that night or that place; it seemed final, officialdom's last word on the subject. I had one chance left, and I took it. I called my friend Mary Anna.

8. The house of young men.

Mary Anna was the most beautiful of my friends. At fourteen she had thick elbow-length hair that rippled slowly outward in waves, green eyes (from colored contact lenses), and a lush, pillowy body that she dressed in velvets and dark, vibrant colors. Mary Anna lived with her artist father in an apartment that was all glass and modern lines. Sculptures of impossibly youthful and lithe male torsos sat on pedestals about the room. Her father had been married to Mary Anna's mother until he recognized that he was gay. There was longing in the torsos he sculpted and something else, too, that made my breath catch when I looked closely at them.

"You can stay here," Mary Anna said, opening the door, "but just for one night." Her father was nowhere to be seen.

I slept that night in the living room, among the silent torsos of beautiful men. They leaned up and away, leaving me floating there, safe in space.

9. Drives.

"Why did you leave?" Tom asked me in the car the next day.

Even then, in the thick of it, his willful stupidity stunned me. Because you threatened to rape me, that's why. But we never used those words, those ugly, realistic words. Even my diary was a carefully kept blank. Tom and all he represented was expressed only by the word "It," with its initial capital letter.

"Because of what you said," I told him instead.

"But you knew I didn't mean it." We were sitting outside my school. When I called that morning to say that I was gone, he insisted on picking me up. I gave in, the way I always gave in, because it was easier. Because I was tired. Because there were no neat lines to be drawn, not between him and me, no matter what I did. I looked at him, his worried brow and slightly graying hair. No, I hadn't known that, and still didn't.

"You must have seen I couldn't stay."

We were already lovers, in some sense, embittered lovers whose affair had gone wrong, taxing each other, fumbling our way through language, each of us convinced of the other's nameless crimes. We had witnesses, even: his wife and son, who had to pretend that the looks between Tom and me, our silences, the way we drew apart when anyone else entered the room, were all normal ways between a man and a child. They did so because they knew. Our continued existence as a family depended on these lies.

He started the car and we drove home, both of us quiet. I had surrendered again, come back to him. He was kind enough not to put into words what we both knew now: that I had nowhere else to go.

10. Nobody killed anybody.

Though that would have made it easier, from my point of view. But Mike and Scotty were just boys, and I was only a girl.

11. The social worker's report.

My social worker was a short, strongly built woman who dressed in power suits before the term had been coined. She seemed faintly repelled by her charges' drug use and sexual adventures, the way we refused to live up to our potential. Of course I'm speculating now. When she first met my foster parents—nice, upper-middle-class people, my foster mother with that promising die-straight part and proper accent, my foster father's bohemianism contained by money and domestic order—she must have been relieved. I, on the other hand, came to her high, smiling at nothing and alluding casually to escapades of which she was bound to disapprove. The running away, my most serious misdemeanor so far, struck her as nothing more than my fear of being punished.

Her report, which I wouldn't see for another year and a half, laid out the script: me the ungrateful daughter, Tom and my foster mother the benevolent liberals opening their home to a child who gave them nothing but grief in return. I had left Tom's house by then. It wasn't the glamorous running away I had envisioned. I'd simply gone to my grandmother's as usual that summer; when it came time to leave, I refused to return. There had been somewhere to go, after all.

I never did present my virginity to Tom. But I had been awakened to its troublesome potential, and I set out to dispose of it as soon as I found a likely candidate. I did not want to possess an item of barter that commanded such a high and painful price.

12. Finished with Tom.
Or was I? I went to visit him once that fall. I had spent the summer in my grandmother's large house on the river, walking through fields, seeing no one. I was like someone whose wound is held together only provisionally, so that it may burst anew at any moment. I had not yet, as they say in social-worker parlance, "disclosed." Tom and my foster mother had moved again. In the new

house, their German shepherd Bear came to the foot of the stairs, sniffed me without much interest, walked upstairs again, then came tearing back down in a ball of fur. He had remembered who I was.

13. Remnants.

Letters and a picture in the mail, Tom's new daughter, her face hardly formed. Years later, a phone call from a hotel room in yet another city. I was on my own by this time, with a conference to attend, a speech to deliver before strangers, an apartment to return to. Yes, I had the right number. Yes, the dog was fine. Could he come and see me? he asked. No, I said, with tears streaming down my face. No, I said to him.

14. Men like Tom.

Once in a while I see a man in the supermarket or on the street whose behavior, as he bends to his girl-child, is far too ardent to be decent. Instantly, I understand who he is, what he wants; my body stiffens at the sight. I recognize in him Tom's heavy breathing, the way his eyes would follow me from the room. I see in the strange man the thrill of possession. I turn away, but what I want, more than anything, is to whisper in the girl-child's small ear: *Be careful. He will try and take you away from yourself.* A warning, for all the good it would do. The one I never got.

Will You Kiss Me?

Marnie Woodrow

Whenever I see a copy of *Cosmopolitan* magazine, I remember how it helped me to figure out what a "real" girl was—and also how it led to my first kiss. First I had to suffer, but the pay-off was worth it.

I got hooked on *Cosmo* when I was fourteen. My mother used to buy it along with other less exciting magazines like *Good Housekeeping* and *Woman's World*. I read them all from cover to cover, including the endless casserole recipes and tips on stain removal. But it was *Cosmopolitan* that I would sneak off to my room to devour. My ongoing obsession with it was like seeing a car accident on the side of the road: you don't want to look, but you just can't tear your eyes away.

The *Cosmo* universe revolved around three things: sex, makeup, and the challenges of being a single, ambitious, thin, well-dressed female in search of the perfect man. The articles on how to lose weight and how to live alone and like it were fascinating in a remote way. The magazine's fixation on sex also attracted me.

Although I hadn't had sex and felt pretty sure I never would, I was reassured to discover that it was indeed the messy, dangerous, and unpleasant experience I had always envisioned. But I think what really drew me in, month after month, was the complete absence of anything that resembled my own life. I wanted to ride my bike, wear jeans nonstop, read poetry, and one day write a book of my own, maybe even a few books. In the *Cosmo* universe, which I ached to be part of, there were no tomboys or artists, just women whose lives seemed to depend on choosing the right shade of lipstick. I reasoned that if I studied the magazine closely enough, I'd somehow magically become a Cosmo Girl, which is to say I'd become a *real* girl and eventually a real woman.

In my first year of high school I was a loner. My parents had just split up, and there was a lot I didn't want people to know about my family. There was a lot I didn't want people to know about me, either, so I kept to myself most of the time. I had some friends, but no one I actually trusted. I had even started to drift away from my mom. Although she was the only person in the world I felt I could count on, I was scared that if I told her the truth about certain things, I'd disappoint her so much she would hate me. I was wrong about that, as it turned out, but at fourteen I wasn't going to gamble.

I wasn't very interested in drugs, or was too afraid to try them, but reading offered me the same kind of escape. I read everything I could get my hands on: books, magazines, dictionaries, even the phone book. I spent hours writing and drawing. And while every other girl in my small hometown was hung up on the sexy male lead singers of various heavy metal bands, I was obsessed with the pop singer Madonna, who was then starting to become famous. I read whatever I could find about her, and my mother's concern about my social isolation wasn't helped by the three hundred-and-counting pictures of Madonna that decorated my bedroom wall.

Towards the end of ninth grade, just as I had lost hope of ever finding a best friend, I met Andrea. She was pretty and popular, wore just the right amount of makeup and sewed her own stylish clothes, and she was blonde. Boys used to call my house trying to get her phone number. I should have hated her for that, but she was also the nicest, funniest, and kindest person I had ever known. And anyway, it wasn't her fault that boys thought I wouldn't mind being her dating service. Although I could talk to them about everything from BMX bikes to baseball, I wasn't the sort of girl a guy would ask out on a date. I didn't think that was such a bad thing, at least not once I met Andrea.

Andrea and I talked about almost everything. Her childhood had been much worse than mine, and like me she was very good at hiding her pain. We would laugh hysterically about the awful things we had seen and experienced. Kind words and encouragement were alien concepts to Andrea, and I was shocked at how badly her parents treated her. Here was this gorgeous, wonderful girl everybody at school wanted to know, and yet all she heard at home was how stupid she was. Andrea seemed to find me as funny and exciting as I found her. I decided to devote my whole being to making her realize what a great person she was. I wrote her poems and did everything I could to make her laugh. Her parents, perhaps sensing that Andrea had an ally in the outside world, began to hate me. I hated them right back, especially when they told Andrea she couldn't see me any more. We got around that one by joining the school theater group, which allowed us to spend lots of time together.

My mom was really happy about Andrea. Having a best friend meant that I stopped going to movies by myself, and that I willingly went to high school dances. I spent less time on my Madonna museum, too. My mom treated Andrea as part of our family, at one point even asking her if she wanted to come live with us. Considering that we had a small apartment and not much money, this invitation meant a lot to Andrea, and to me.

I still read *Cosmopolitan* religiously, and my favorite feature was an advice column written by Irma Kurtz. Women would write in asking for help with everything from bad breath and jealous boyfriends to strained relations with their best friends. I read every letter and studied Irma's responses, hoping to learn from other people's dumb mistakes. Unfortunately, though, none of the best-friend dilemmas were the same as the one I was experiencing: I sometimes caught myself wanting to kiss Andrea. I fervently hoped those thoughts would go away before she figured it out. I was pretty certain that I was a total freak, since none of the letters in Irma Kurtz's column were from women who wanted to kiss other women.

Today you can type the word "lesbian" into an Internet search engine and instantly confirm that there are lots of gay and bisexual women out there. But this was the early 1980s. All I had to go on was the surprising revelation (delivered in passing) that my mother had gone to nursing school with a *lesbian*. This shocking news prompted me to look up the word in my always-useful dictionary. "Lesbian: *n.* a female homosexual." Not exactly the kind of help I was looking for. And even if I wasn't the only such girl in the world, I was sure I was the only one in my hometown.

I had often composed letters to the all-knowing Irma Kurtz in my head, but now my questions took on a greater urgency.

Dear Irma,

I am a teenage girl who needs your help. I desperately want to care about yeast infections and other feminine things. I want to have the courage to pluck my eyebrows without screaming and to figure out how not to feel totally stupid in a dress. I want to learn how to have an affair with my boss without risking my job (when I finally have a job and a boss to go with it). And although I don't think I'm fat, I would like to at least worry about it like everybody else does. In other words, I want to be a real girl. Is there some way to make this happen, or should I just wait for a miracle?

Another thing that's bugging me is that I sometimes want to kiss my best friend. I mean really *kiss her. I'd rather not have a sex change operation, because then I'd have to move away and change my name and buy new clothes. And I don't actually want to be a man. Please help!*

Signed,

Terminal Tomboy

P.S. I think I get along with guys too well. If they ask me to do something I say yes (if I feel like it) or no (if I don't), and I can see from Cosmo *that this is the wrong approach. How can I become confusing and mysterious so guys will think I'm sexy?*

From time to time I experimented with makeup, standing in front of the bathroom mirror for hours because I knew it was my duty as a potential real girl to do so. My efforts to imitate a movie star always failed, but I did have fun making myself look like someone whose face had been torn apart by zombies. At school and elsewhere I was often mistaken for a guy, and I was sure the reason for that was my thick eyebrows. I tried plucking them, but I ended up with a big hole in the middle of one and two patches of skin that felt as if they had been attacked by killer bees. It seemed to me that beauty involved more physical pain than I was up for. I resigned myself to being ugly, despite my mother's assurances that I was beautiful and had a "wonderful figure"—whatever that meant.

All this time I was crazy in love with Andrea. I was sure that telling her would mean the end of our friendship forever. But I felt like I would go nuts if I kept it a secret. I also felt like a liar and a creep because we spent so much time together and slept in the same bed and saw each other naked. So one night I broke down and told her—and not very directly, I might add. I bet people have had an easier time decoding the Riddle of the Sphinx! But when she figured out what I was saying, she said of course she didn't hate me. She hugged me and said that she was proud of me for being so honest and brave. Whew. Her response didn't erase my feelings, but it was a huge relief to know that we could still be friends even after I'd told her the truth. (That isn't always how life works, but when it does, it's incredible.)

Even though I spent almost every waking minute either thinking about Andrea or talking to her, I was careful to keep up with my reading because Andrea liked the fact that I was bookish and, in her opinion, "smart." We had decided that I was going to become a famous poet. Everyone knows that in addition to being an expert on English literature, a real poet must also know everything there is to know about sex, so one afternoon at the public library I decided to skip the poetry section and head straight for Health and Fitness. As I had discovered on another day of deeply studious exploration, this was where the librarian stashed the sex books.

Glancing around to make sure no one was watching me, I picked a likely candidate from the shelf, *The Big Book of Sex for Girls and Boys* or some embarrassing title like that. I began to flip through it, depressed by the diagrams of penises and bored with the lengthy section on menstruation. I was about to give up when my eyes fell upon the word "lesbian." I froze, then glanced over my shoulder again, but nobody seemed to be looking my way. The book had a bibliography, and I scanned it. One of the titles listed was a novel called *The Well of Loneliness* by Radclyffe Hall.

I reshelved the sex book and hurried off. But all the way home I kept thinking about this Radclyffe Hall person, wondering why a guy would write a book about lesbians. Even though I doubted that my small-town library would have such a novel in its collection, I knew I had to look it up. I went back to the library the very next day after school, and I was amazed: they *did* have it. Heart pounding, I located the book in the stacks, then disappeared with it into a back corner of the library, praying that I wouldn't run into anyone I knew. At that time, libraries still used a manual system for checking books out; a card kept in an envelope glued to the first page of each book was stamped whenever the book was borrowed. When I looked at the card in the front of *The Well of Loneliness*, I gasped. Someone else had signed it out!

My mouth was dry as I read the introduction to the novel. It was old, published in 1928. And Radclyffe Hall was a woman! How had she had the guts to write such a thing so long ago? And who was the other lesbian in town who had borrowed it? I shoved the book back onto the shelf, but once I got home I couldn't stop thinking about it. The introduction had said that although the book was banned at first, a bunch of famous writers protested until it was made accessible to the public. If somebody was brave enough to write a book about being a lesbian, the least I could do was be brave enough to sign it out.

I went back to the library again the next afternoon, hoping the librarian would attribute my increasingly frequent visits to my deep love of literature. I stood around in the fiction section for a bit trying to summon up my courage. Finally, I took a deep breath, yanked *The Well of Loneliness* down from the shelf and hurried to the sign-out desk with the front cover pressed to my sweatshirt. There was no way the librarian could know the story line of every book in the place. And nobody would know who'd signed the novel out once I managed to get it home. A part of me liked the danger of it all. I loved the idea of sitting up late in my room with a once-banned book in my hands. Madonna would be proud, I told myself. I tried to look calm and cool as the librarian stamped my card and wished me a nice afternoon.

I could barely contain my excitement as I sat through dinner that night. I excused myself from the table as soon as I could without arousing my mom's suspicions and rushed to my room, where *The Well of Loneliness* waited in its hiding place at the back of a drawer. I kept an ear out for footsteps approaching my door as I opened what I felt was going to be the best book of all time.

By the time I was a few chapters into it, I was more depressed than I'd been in my entire life. One of the main characters, the lover of the tale, goes by a man's name and dresses like a man when she is courting her female beloved. My heart sank. It was just as I had feared. Everyone in the book was happy except the lesbian. She was a freak, and that meant that I was one, too. How long would it be before I was wearing tuxedos and marching around in a fedora, trying to trick women into loving me? I was positive now that I was destined for a life full of unrequited crushes and silent suffering. I closed the book, unable to continue reading.

I'd told Andrea about signing out *The Well of Loneliness*. When she asked me about it a few days later, I confessed my misery.

"But Marnie," she said, "you're not like that. You're beautiful as a girl. I'm sure that isn't the only way to be a lesbian."

"I *hate* that word!" I exclaimed in despair. "I'm never going to call myself that, ever. It sounds like a skin disease! Forget it. I'm just going to be a nothing for the rest of my life."

A few weeks later, I was whipping up a late-night snack for Andrea and me at my house. My mom was out on a date, so we had the place to ourselves. I loved it when that happened, because in my mind it was almost as good as having my own apartment. My mom wasn't in the habit of leaving me alone very often, so I tried to make the most of it when she did, lighting candles and playing my music a little louder than usual. Andrea sat on a chair, watching me prepare the feast. She seemed kind of quiet that night, not as responsive to my jokes. I tried not to let it bother me as I busied myself with the pots and pans. All of a sudden Andrea was beside me, handing me a note. That was odd, because we weren't in class. I looked at her.

"Just read it," she said, staring at the floor.

I unfolded the piece of paper with shaky hands and read the note. *Will you kiss me?* it said.

I thought I would have a heart attack right there in the kitchen. I kept my eyes on Andrea's handwriting because my face was burning. *Will you kiss me?* I read it over and over. Was it a joke? A dream? I was afraid to look at Andrea, as if that might make her change her mind. But finally I had to look up.

"Answer it!" she said, her face turning pink. I realized she was serious. And nervous too.

I grabbed a pen and wrote *YES* on the note in big letters and handed it back. I could hardly breathe. I was sure I had died and this was heaven, where the things you dreamed of actually came true. I didn't even care if, right after kissing her, I died for real. That's how much I wanted that kiss.

I had read a lot of stuff in my life, but nothing quite as thrilling and scary as those words. That note opened up a whole new world for me. A world where I didn't have to wear men's clothes in order for a beautiful, I mean *really* beautiful, girl to ask me to kiss her. A girl who made my knees weak. That I was a girl too did not seem to matter to her.

I did kiss Andrea, of course. It was everything I had imagined it would be: exciting, terrifying, romantic. Sexy, even. After all those times of trying not to stare at her mouth, of trying not to love her "that way," I was kissing her. *And she was kissing me back!* In that moment I knew that *Cosmo* had been wrong.

You see, the more I read about makeovers and crash diets

and choosing the perfect hairstyle, the farther away I seemed to get from becoming a "real" girl. The more I explored the concepts of "turning him on" and "keeping him guessing," the less I wanted to do either thing. *Cosmopolitan* magazine didn't make me a tomboy or a lesbian or an artist. I was already all those things, in a reluctant sort of way. I had originally hoped the magazine would help me learn to be different. In fact, the opposite happened.

For a while I thought that Radclyffe Hall was wrong, too, but later I realized she was simply telling her story, just as I am telling you mine. She was describing one way that gay women of her time managed to find love and romance. They dressed in men's clothes partly for practical reasons (camouflage) and partly for fun.

I guess I always knew there was something more out there, and reading helped me find it: a magazine, a book, and then a bravely written note. I'd believed I was going to have to wait to start my life, that I would simply read (and read and read) until it happened. That it happened *while* I was reading was a very cool thing indeed.

Although I refuse to buy it, I still read *Cosmo* now and again. It reminds me of who I am . . . and of who I thought I wanted to be. Maybe I'm sentimental, but I still have those Madonna pictures, too. Madonna has always encouraged outrageous, independent behavior in women. People thought she was hot—even with those bushy eyebrows!

Home

Madeleine Thien

I moved away from home when I was eighteen. In the middle of the day, my boyfriend came in a blue Honda and loaded my books and clothes into the trunk of his car. Leaving was irresponsible: I had no furniture, no money. My mother was angry with me, but it made no difference. When the Honda pulled out of the gravel parking lot, the sun was bright in the sky. We drove west, onto the highway, light glinting off the windshield and the fenders of the cars alongside us. I could see the log booms floating on the river, the industrial smokestacks lining the shore, the subdivisions cut into the hillside—images I had seen my entire life. Music flooded from the radio. I stared out the window, overcome with relief.

As a child, I loved the day-to-day rituals of my family's life. Every morning, while my father made breakfast, I watched from the kitchen table. Chaos reigned all around me—my mother, searching high and low for her purse; my brother, stomping this way and that in his big white running shoes; my sister, frowning, looking nervously for a misplaced notebook. From the stove, my father called out suggestions or reprimands: "Must you walk so heavily? Are you an elephant or a boy?"; "I told you to find your books last night"; and to me, "Eat. Don't daydream." He and my mother spoke Chinese interspersed with English. In our house, a river of language ran through the rooms.

Dinner was the main event. My father would wash the rice and then set the pot in the cooker. I stood guard, listening to the gurgle and hiss of the machine. At the stove, my father moved through smoke and sound, emerging with a plate of vegetables, a whole fish, a pot of chicken soup. My mother, in the background, gathered us up and set the table. When we sat down together, all the chattering faded and we ate in silence, the food holding our attention. Our dining room was wallpapered with a blown-up photograph of the Rocky Mountains, so we devoured roast duck and Shanghai noodles in the shade of those snow-capped peaks.

Afterwards, stuffed, we collapsed in the living room. The volume on the six o'clock news turned low, my parents speaking from time to time, a burst of laughter, then quiet as we settled into evening.

When I was small, the world was colossal. I remember the first movie I saw at a theater—*The Neverending Story*. I can no longer recall the plot, except to say that it begins with a young boy who somehow enters a book. As I watched, I felt myself ricochet from one precipice to another. The images were grand, the music ear-splitting. I was filled with awe.

Real life seemed that way, too. My parents inspired wonder in me. Sitting in the passenger seat of our van, I was enthralled by the assurance of my mother's small hands on the steering wheel as she maneuvered us through traffic. She took me to her office once, and such was her popularity there that we attracted a crowd of onlookers. By the time we were ready to leave, her coworkers had deluged me with candy. Boxes of chocolate candies, a giant bag of caramels. In her wool skirt and sheer nylons, with her dazzling smile, my mother was a sight to behold. Taking my hand, she waved everyone back, then gathered my loot for a quick getaway.

My father was most comfortable in the kitchen. He stood at the counter, cleaver in hand, shearing vegetables and meat. When he fried them in chili and garlic and oil, the room filled with smells so good I danced around him, impatient for a taste. My father was a restrained man. Impassively, he gave me sticks of satay dipped in rich peanut sauce, pastries filled with curry, a bowl of shaved ice topped with lichee fruit and sweet syrup. When he spoke, his voice was gentle and wry.

At this age, our dreams were also colossal. My brother wanted to run the hundred-meter dash in the Olympics. My sister wanted to dance in the National Ballet. I wanted to be Harriet the Spy, to sit in a dumbwaiter and eavesdrop. I wanted to find the wardrobe that would allow me to enter Narnia.

When I was seven, the bank foreclosed on my parents' mortgage, and we lost our house. One morning moving trucks appeared on the street out front. Two burly movers whisked our belongings away while my father hovered in the background, his face drawn. I stayed with him that evening when my mother took my brother and sister to our new apartment. We cleaned the house, moving from room to room with a cloth, wiping the marks from the walls. Afterwards, we sat on the back steps, and I held his hand as he stared at the lawn and the trees. "We have lost everything," he said to me in despair.

In the years that followed, we moved frequently, trying to find a place we could afford on my family's dwindling income. Under the financial strain, my parents' marriage began to crumble. There were no real arguments, but a heavy silence descended on our home. The tension eventually flowed around all of us, like water between rocks. My brother and sister, busy with work and school, barely came home. It seemed to me that I woke up one morning and the unthinkable had happened. No longer did we sit down together at the kitchen table, captivated by my father's delicious meals. Instead, he cooked dinner in the late afternoon and left it on the stove. One by one, we helped ourselves, carrying our plates to the television or to our bedrooms. Eating in solitude, and increasingly living our lives that way.

My brother was the first to leave. He was seventeen, the oldest child and the most tempestuous. When he exploded in a rage, my sister and I would flee. His anger seemed to have no limits. He broke furniture, punched the walls, shouted so loudly the neighbors refused to look at us.

One day, as he and my mother fought over his curfew, my brother drove his fist into the closet door. We heard the wood split. Aghast, my mother stumbled from the room, whispering, "Are you crazy? You must be crazy." After he left, storming out with a canvas bag of clothes, my sister and I examined the door. His fist had sailed straight through, past splinters and fragments, clear to the other side.

I was twelve years old, and I loved my parents with a child's devotion. I went to my mother and held her. She wrapped her arms around me. I wanted her to know that I would never injure her as my brother had. It was inconceivable to me that our relationship might someday change. My sense of self was so tied up with my mother and father that I could not imagine a separate existence.

But as I grew older, my feelings changed. My family's faults seemed magnified, and I began to yearn for what we had never had—a comfortable existence, a life free from worries about money. Distracted by their own troubles, my parents did not discipline me or impose any restrictions on my behavior. In some ways I was glad of it, this freedom to act like an adult. I wanted control over my life. But at the same time, I felt as if I were lost in a tempest, turned every which way. There was no one to whom I could turn for guidance. I became impatient with my mother and father, angry that they could not provide me with what I needed.

When I was fifteen I got a job at a nearby McDonald's, working the drive-thru. I'd sit up in a little booth, wearing a headset, and watch the slow parade of cars coming by—rowdy teenagers;

working people, their faces lined and exhausted. The families were my favorite, with their ravenous children. They peered up at me, small faces pressed against the window in delight.

Sometimes I worked until midnight. Afterwards, I would set off alone through the dark, unlit streets. Cars slowed and followed me, men leaning out the window whistling. I would keep walking, past Second Avenue, where the prostitutes waited by lamp posts, smoke from their cigarettes weaving ribbons in the dark. I would keep walking, with my head up, all the way home.

Once, in a fit of dangerous impulse, I got into a car that was following me. The man drove in circles around the city but eventually dropped me at home. When I got out of the car, unharmed, I was weak and shaking. All the lights were off in our apartment, and my parents were sound asleep. I stood in the living room listening to the night sounds, the hush of traffic, the murmuring of a television in my sister's bedroom. A part of me wanted to disappear, to teach my mother and father a lesson. I wanted something terrible to happen so that they would wake from their distraction and see me. But as much as I tried to deny it, as much as it hurt, I knew I could not depend on them. There was only myself to hold onto.

At that age, my favorite poem was by John Donne. It was a love poem, with the image of two lovers as the arms of a compass. One arm holding steady in the center, the other free to roam. How beautiful, I thought. I, too, longed to be held steady, by love or family—in the end, perhaps they would be the same thing for me.

But I also saw the image this way: home as the long arm in the center holding me distant while I circled round and round, yearning to be let inside.

I was sixteen when my father left. One day, I came home from school and walked into his bedroom, looking for him. But as soon as I entered, I knew he was gone. He had taken his clothes. Everything else was left behind—a desk still holding papers and business cards, a cardboard box filled to the brim with black-and-white photographs. My father had left a note telling us he'd gone back to East Malaysia, to the town where he was born.

I did not even know if I should grieve. In the last few years, my parents had been so miserable together, and my father, who had grown up in the heat and humidity of Malaysia, had never considered this country his home. A part of me was glad for him, glad he had taken this risk and left us. I sat down on his bed, thinking that perhaps I would never see him again. Maybe I would grow old and move far away and he would never again be part of my life. At the time, I could not comprehend how a person could so suddenly, so easily, disappear.

We did not hear from my father in the months that followed. My mother, who had always been strong, simply continued. She got up and went to work the next day, and the next, worked away the sorrow and the disappointment. My sister and I followed her lead. We went on too, hardly pausing to discuss it. In hindsight, our behavior strikes me as odd. But my parents' marriage had been in a shambles for so many years that by the time decisive action was taken, it felt like a door closing long after the house itself had been abandoned.

Nights when my mother came home late from work, her clothes wrinkled and loose on her, her eyes circled with shadows, I dreamed of a life apart from my family. I wanted to live fearlessly, so I behaved that way—late nights, fast driving, unprotected sex. I also began stealing regularly. A pair of earrings, a scarf, a blue felt pen—anything that caught my eye. I'd hold it in my hand, then make it vanish. When I finally wandered home, my mother would lose her temper, rage about my irresponsibility, my recklessness, but her anger could no longer touch me. She saw our family unravelling, and she was desperate to hold things together. But for me, the disintegration had already happened. I was buoyed by my independence. At the end of each day, I poured my thoughts into a journal. If in my regular life I was calm and unrevealing, here I let loose, my dreams and longings skidding across the page.

Once, I asked permission to go to a concert in Seattle. My mother forbade it. I ignored her and drove off that afternoon in a car packed with teenagers. After the concert, I watched fireworks burn up in the July night. My life seemed like that, a split second of beauty and then nothing—just waste and debris falling in darkness.

My mother was furious when I returned. While she lectured, I sat on the couch unmoved. She shook my shoulders, begging me to listen, but I refused. I was no longer the devoted child, and all my parents' missteps, their losses and failures, seemed so pathetically clear to me. I would not let my life be like theirs, a constant struggle for money and love and security.

I think my mother believed that I was lost. Certainly, I was lost to her. We could not carry on a conversation, because I instantly drifted out of it. "Are you taking drugs?" she asked me once. I remember laughing, the idea was so ludicrous. There were a million things that could ruin you. But the first, I thought, was home. If that did not hold you steady, you would be compelled to run.

My sister was the next to leave. She and my mother fought continually, and one night she moved her belongings out while we slept. In the morning, her bedroom was empty.

Even as a child, I loved the city where we lived, the grid of streets and alleys, the electrical wires running like seams through the neighborhoods. In the abandoned lots, weeds and dandelions bloomed among the pebbles. My sister and I had walked here together, but now I walked alone, late at night, after my mother had fallen asleep. I knew how each street curved into the next, the way Kingsway cut its diagonal across Slocan, how Knight Street swerved dangerously into Clark. In my head, I could list the streets off one by one, thirty or forty at a time, east to west.

Once, when we were younger, my sister had told me she dreamed of running away. But she worried that every place would be the same, a never-ending line of houses with only convenience stores and shopping malls to vary the landscape. The same person, always disappointed, thumping along behind her. I understood her perfectly. Unlike my father, we yearned to leave home behind. When his marriage collapsed and his family fell apart, he returned to the landscape he had once known intimately. As if home, the home of his memory, could help him set his life on course again.

When I moved away from home I did not leave in the night, as my sister had, or after a fit of violence, as my brother had. I did not step into an airplane that would take me away from the life I knew.

Instead, I responded to an ad for a live-in nanny. A woman named Antoinette, who lived near the university, was looking for someone to take care of her daughter five nights a week. In exchange, I would receive free room and board.

My mother shook her head at me. "You think you know how to take care of yourself. You think it will be so easy. But you don't have a clue what it's like to be on your own." Her disapproval only strengthened my resolve.

The room that I moved into was small and square: a mattress on the floor, a table, a telephone. I unpacked in minutes. When I was done, the room was still spartan.

Downstairs, I could hear Antoinette putting the groceries away. Her kitchen was filled with foods I had never encountered at home—bagels, cream cheese, perogies, antipasto. Gone were the large bags of rice, the oyster sauce, the dried Chinese mushrooms and packets of sugar cane. The change that I had yearned for was beginning with something as particular, as basic, as food.

That first night, I called my mother. Her voice on the phone was scratchy and distant. We exchanged pleasantries, and then there was a long, uncomfortable silence. I pictured her alone in the townhouse, surrounded by empty space. "Is it strange having the place to yourself?" I asked her.

"Strange?" She paused. "I suppose it is. But you always know it will happen, the kids grow up and move on. I'll get used to it eventually." She stopped, as if weighing her words. "You might move back."

"I don't think so."

"You'd be welcome."

I laughed, feeling old suddenly with my mother. "You might regret saying that."

"Yes," she said, laughing too. "I might."

"But I'll remember."

"Good." Her voice was kind. "Be careful."

"I will."

That night, my boyfriend asleep beside me, I thought of my mother, the one who had never left. Through all the comings and goings, she had stayed, as steady as the compass arm in the center.

A year later, I rode in a plane for the first time. It was a six-seater that rattled as it soared over farmlands, the city below stretching along the coast. Thousands of feet above ground, I climbed underneath the wing, perching precariously on a little ledge. A hand tapped the small of my back, and I let go. Free fall. Ten seconds, watching my arms and legs dart away from my body. Then the chute opened, an echoing shot. I hung there, suspended in the blue sky. I thought I could see to the ends of the earth. For a moment, I felt I could set myself down anywhere.

Someone told me recently that my mother and I have the same laugh. I wondered, What else? What else do we share that I've failed to notice? After my father left, she spoke about him only once, looking up from her work to say, "I tried, I really did." Then she asked, "Was I such a poor wife?" I shook my head, not knowing how to answer. Now, I try to imagine my mother as a sixteen-year-old girl, dreaming of an unconventional life. She risked everything and came to North America. She made this place her home in a way that my father never could.

For her, this is the place that remains, despite a sea change. My mother understands home, holds her hands around it in a way that I still do not quite understand. When she was fifty, she finally bought her own house, surprising even herself. I hope for the same, for time to reinvent myself, to evolve the way a story changes, stops and circles back, building on its own impetus. Change can be so blinding, so complete, that the distance from my age now, twenty-six, to thirty-five might be as vast as the distance I once imagined ahead of me to twenty. Wonderful, I think. To always be surprised. To come to know home in an unforeseen way, different from anything I can now imagine.

Nerves Out Loud

M K Quednau

Dear Bud:

It feels funny to call you that. Back then it was always "Mr. Allison." At least to your face. Behind your back we would whisper, "Hey look, there's Bud." You were the only teacher we knew with a nickname. But you were kind of different anyway. You were just yourself.

Some of my friends would laugh at you for walking down the halls with your eyes glued to an open book, mumbling and bumping into kids by their lockers; you were off in your own little world. We'd say, "He's probably reading Wordsworth." And then we would imitate your serious, strumming voice reading aloud: "If solitude, or fear, or pain, or grief / Should be thy portion—"

But we all admired you. I guess I saw a little of myself in the way you seemed surprised to exist in this world at all. Like you had to slip in and out of some real time and place. I knew the feeling. Still do. I have to pinch myself sometimes. High school mostly seems thousands of years behind me now, like some strong wind blew all the people from that time away. I get a taste in my mouth that's salty and black, like the root of something, like licorice. It's the taste of absence.

On rare days, if I press hard for the memories, I can still get there. Flash back to some vivid scene from Emery Collegiate, stuck high up on that windy hill. Like good old Mr. Mortimer, the Vice-P, looking on with disbelief at the half-dozen girls hoisted on the boys' shoulders in that jousting game we used to play. We ended up laughing our heads off, all of us piled up in a tangle of bodies on the school's front lawn.

Poor Mort; he probably thought our double-decker games would lead to teenage pregnancy or something. I remember him saying that we were too old for such childishness, that with the girls wearing such short skirts, well, we should behave with more "decorum." I muttered that if girls were allowed to wear jeans, like the boys, it wouldn't be a problem. Of course that earned me a detention.

That's the kind of thing I used to shoot off my mouth about. Small prickly moments of what felt like injustice. Besides, when Mort asked us to "settle down," we only ended up in the smoke pit again, down by the bus stop. I'm sure that wasn't the kind of "grown-up" behavior he'd intended. This was before anyone knew for certain that smoking could kill you; it just "looked bad." But even if I'd known the dangers, I'd have inhaled a few packs anyway. In those days I didn't feel I had a lot to lose.

I got a ton of detentions, I know that. Had to carry some from the ninth grade to the tenth, which wasn't exactly elegant. I always seemed to be verging on rude. Or to be laughing at the wrong times. From sheer nervousness, I think now. Nerves out loud, that was me. Or maybe I blurted things out from a sense of irony. You taught us about that, "Irony and All Its Uses." But let's face it, I already had a hunch. *Life is absurd*, my bones used to sing. *Everything young is old*, I often wanted to say. *Everything right is wrong. Everything alive is dead, and the dead still raise their voices.*

You were the only one who seemed to understand. While others were forcing Latin declensions or the history of H₂O down our throats, you were the one granting me permission. You were actually *encouraging* me to write poems about death. You knew how ancient the world was and how it kept on spinning, all of us getting older every minute of every day. I could hear it in my own heartbeat and in the regular shuffle, shuffle, shuffle of all those people in the halls. I sometimes wanted to shout, "What's the point? Why are we all going back and forth, back and forth?"

And then I would write myself a poem and it would grow light and silent in my head, crystal clear for a change. Writing a poem was what I ended up doing a lot of the time. In physics, or in the gym change room, and especially in Mrs. Winter's class (aka Mrs. Ants-in-her-pants). I can never forget that hectic look on her face, like it was an emergency to "finish our assignments." I can still hear the chairs screeching on the floor and Mrs. Antsy's high-pitched, frantic voice telling us to sit down. She was always telling us to stop our "chit-chat" and start "expanding our minds."

She didn't exactly inspire us to listen, not like you had. You were probably the first and last time a lot of kids actually liked English class. All you had to do was open a book and everyone wiggling in their seats or dropping pens or whispering at the back of the room would get quiet. You would just start reading, as though you cared about every word on the page. And we would care too. Plus, you told us things that mattered, how the poet William Blake had visions, and how writers could see into the future, like fortune-tellers.

Mrs. Antsy was a real shock to the system; with her, English became a lot of rules about commas and sentence fragments. The worst time was when she wanted us to write that letter. I knew it was one of those exercises teachers invented to keep students busy.

We were supposed to imagine writing to someone famous, like the Queen or Ed Sullivan. Or maybe Beethoven. I don't remember if it had to be somebody alive. Just that it was really an essay in disguise, and that essays were intended to convince someone of something.

Mrs. A was probably getting desperate and thought in this roundabout way she might yet inspire us to greatness. "Surely there's someone you admire," she said when she looked over my shoulder and noticed the blank white page. She sounded edgy, like there had better be a hero in my life, and fast. "Not really," I said. In those days I didn't think the Beatles would make it big. Or that a man named Neil Armstrong would soon walk on the moon. I had my reasons to hold back.

I tried to think of one single person who inspired me, some-one brave or brilliant, a famous inventor or movie star. But my brain stubbornly refused to dream up any celebrity. Instead, I thought of my mother then, whose name I couldn't even mention out loud at that time, or for years afterward. My mother, who was too shiny and bright in my head, like a martyr or a saint. Thinking of my mother, and not being able to think of her, well, that meant I couldn't do it. Write the letter. It was as simple as that.

I'm not sure I understood what "admire" actually meant. If it was at all like love. And I didn't have a clear concept of what love was, either. I was all mixed up in those days about whether loving someone always ended in tragedy.

Apparently it wasn't a good time of my life to be feeling this way. Aunt Alice looked worried about me sometimes. That's where I was living "for the time being," with her and Uncle Duncan. She said I should comb my hair when I left for school, that I shouldn't say "no" so quickly to any boy who asked me out. That I might be "falling in love" anytime soon.

I didn't know what to say to her. Even the prospect of "falling" wasn't such good news. And I couldn't think of anyone who would be falling with me. All I could see in my head was a jumble of arms and legs, and a boy's face and a girl's face (mine) and our catapulting down a long flight of stairs. And at first we were laughing and then we were crying, because it hurt so much to fall so long and hard; and finally it was quiet at the bottom, with a girl and a boy lying very, very still. Like my mother when I last saw her. With my father.

Now, why would I ever choose to have this happen? This crazy picture of ending up in a heap, me and some boy in so-called love, both of us as heavy and sad as could be? It didn't make sense. Of course nothing did back then. School was everything or nothing. It really mattered what my friends thought and what marks I got, or else it didn't matter at all. I couldn't decide. Christmas was coming that year as slow as ever, with snow everywhere and a dead kind of calm, or else it was rushing past like a giant wind full of people's faces. I couldn't get anything straight.

What I do remember is fiddling with my pen for the longest time in that stale-aired room, the hour ticking away on that fateful day, and Mrs. Antsy tiptoeing up and down the aisles to see how we were "progressing." I used to hate the squeaking of her sensible rubber-soled shoes. By the time the bell rang, I had scribbled only a few sentences on my foolscap: "So you pooh-poohed the fear in your life, as Aunt Alice said the other day. And took your children and packed up three suitcases of things collected over twenty-five years of a fierce loyalty to a man and a house and said good-bye to fear. And fear followed you."

That's all I handed in, placing my shabby attempt on Mrs. A's desk and heading like a sprinter for the door. But Mrs. Antsy stopped me. She looked at me sternly. "Pooh-poohed isn't a real word," she said. I burst out laughing because she sounded so earnest. "And to whom is this letter addressed? We don't really know."

I wanted to say, "My letter is addressed to Beauty." That's what I thought English class was supposed to be about; finding beauty and finding the right words. And I couldn't help thinking of my mother, even with the bruises on her face, even with the sadness in her eyes. In her last staff photo (she was a teacher too, of Art and English, in a school outside the city) she looked radiant. She was surrounded by that light people had in old oil paintings from the Middle Ages. People about to die.

I had been reading a lot about dying, I remember. I suppose I have you, Bud, to thank for that. All the books you loaned me, all those late nights with my head buried in some poem or story about death; the subject drew me like a magnet, felt as familiar as my own life. It was like building muscles or growing immune; after a while I found I could look straight at people who said to me, "It's too bad what happened in your family, it's so tragic, blah blah blah." I could almost *look right through them,* then smile in that upside-down way that wasn't exactly convincing, even to myself. It was a sad smile.

Sometimes I think I scared people. Like the time we were supposed to be picking subjects for debate. The suggested topics were "Plastics in the Home" and "The Population Explosion: Our Planet's Future." Not exactly sizzlers. Right out of the blue, I said, "What about murder-suicide?" The words just popped out of me.

There was this long strained silence. Then Mrs. Antsy said, all bright and cheery, as though we were talking about Christmas decorations or something, "Why, that's an intriguing subject."

If I had been *her* teacher, I would have said to her right then and there, "Think, Mrs. Winter. Is *intriguing* really the right word? Does it adequately express what you wanted to say?"

Instead, she had to remind me that she was still *my* teacher. She asked, "Do you think you're up to all the research?"

"Already done it," I assured her. She was struck dumb for an answer.

I wanted to show her I knew what I was talking about. "For example, did you know that home is the most dangerous place to be? After a marriage breaks up, that's when people take drastic measures. Mostly men, and mostly with guns. So that leaves the victims to be mainly women and children. That's pretty grim, eh?"

Mrs. Antsy was moving her mouth like a goldfish, but no sound was coming out. "Half the time these murders in the family follow a history of domestic violence: that's social-worker talk for fighting viciously, like your life depends on it."

I was starting to get panicked by the silence in the room. But I couldn't stop myself. "And did you realize that men commit suicide more often than women? But when women decide to—they prefer pills or drowning. Isn't that weird? I found all that out just by phoning the national department of statistics."

"What will be the two sides to the debate?" Mrs. Antsy asked finally, in a faint voice. She was looking at me like I was a bomb that might explode at any minute. Even some of the kids in the class were kind of spooked. Still, everyone, including me, wanted to see what would happen next. Our typically snoring-boring English class was being cranked up a notch.

I said I hadn't figured out the exact questions for debate, and would get back to her on it. I just thought it was a neat subject and would lead to a lot of discussion afterward, which was always the sign of a good topic. She had said so herself.

My little outburst led Mrs. A to suggest I see the guidance counsellor. It's funny that I don't remember his name, only his very thick glasses and his very orange socks. Pumpkin-colored. He asked me in his wanna-be-calm voice what I wanted to become when I grew up. When I shrugged and looked uncertain, he kept handing me leaflets with pictures of secretaries and stewardesses and nurses with painted-on eyebrows and little white uniforms.

I couldn't work up much enthusiasm for his suggestions. When he asked me what I was thinking about—would I like to talk about it?—I asked him why he wore those orange socks. I said some of the kids made fun of him, but that I thought he might be a "free spirit" or a "rebel." I remember rolling those words around in my mouth for effect. I figured that could have been an icebreaker between us. Might have led to some real insights or at least a more convincing conversation. But Mr. Socks only smiled bleakly and looked down at his feet. Never said another word.

The theme of my doubtful future stuck to me like glue. "What do you want to be when you grow up?" Mr. Algebra asked me after school. He had a long unpronounceable name with a lot of x's and y's, like an equation, and was rumored to be a genius. I was barely passing math, mostly ducked down my head in his class and wrote scraps of poems. It was just my bad luck he happened to be supervising detentions.

"I think I'll be a teacher," I said impulsively. He had that look of fractions in his eyes, that look of oranges and apples and how many sections make a whole. I could smell another detention in the air. "I'm not joking," I insisted. "Maybe even a math teacher."

He made me write it one hundred times: *When I grow up, I want to be a math teacher.* Some of the writing got pretty wobbly towards the end, because I was in a hurry to get out of there.

My hand was cramping pretty badly by the time I was finished. So I made a big deal of shaking it while he actually counted the lines. I guess I got fidgety, because that's when I had a brilliant afterthought. "Or maybe a writer. I think I might become a writer."

Obviously I wasn't supposed to change my mind. I had to repeat that idea ninety-nine more times on paper: *When I grow up, I think I might become a writer.* After scribbling the sentence over and over, the idea started to appeal to me. I had never actually linked the writing of my desperate poems to any sort of career. But why not? Why shouldn't I become a writer?

Mr. Algebra rose from his chair and reminded me I had to hurry and pack up, or I would miss the last bus. He was big on keeping track of time. And I wanted to leave, but I could see he hadn't taken me seriously. "I want to become a writer because in some countries, poets and novelists are locked away for their shocking thoughts," I explained. "And I would gladly go to prison for saying things I believe."

He must have thought I was pushing some point, and maybe

I was. He shook his head and returned his bulging briefcase to the desk in the now-empty room. Everyone else had gone.

"Sit down, young lady. And write the following: *I would gladly go to prison for saying things I believe.*" I was ten lines into the assignment, hunched over the paper, when he sighed heavily. "And when you're finished, you will have to phone your parents to get a ride home. The bus will have gone by then."

"I don't have any parents," I said to Mr. Algebra. Surely he couldn't blame *that* on me. I couldn't see getting another detention for that huge smudge on my life.

"They, uh . . . passed away." He looked horrified, as if I was making it up or something. So I added, "Quite recently. They died quite recently."

I remember thinking it was odd that he'd forgotten this pertinent fact about me. I thought everybody knew about what had happened. That there was somehow a shame to it, a vague blaming that might involve me. That I was tainted by the event, like having a head too big for my body or an aura of blue strobing light. I thought the heavy metallic sound of death crashed around in everyone else's head like it did in mine.

We both must have looked surprised. I think it started to dawn on him then: this was *real,* not just some invention of mine. It had really happened. By this time I was getting an angry rash on my cheeks—I could feel the heat spreading—and my Shetland wool sweater felt itchy as hell. I blinked back the salt in my eyes and let him have it. The straight goods. "It was in a snowstorm, on a road. Except it wasn't an accident with a car or anything. It involved a gun. And if you want me to, I'll write it all down a thousand times."

Mr. Algebra ended up calling me a taxi and paying for it out of his own pocket. He looked so pale I felt a little sorry for him.

The next morning I was called in to see the guidance counsellor first thing. I thought maybe Mr. Orange Socks had reconsidered how we might both be misfits and kindred spirits after all. He actually seemed interested in me. "So I gather you want to become an Author?" He made it sound so stuffy and formal.

Well, the thought had occurred to me, I admitted, because I often had something to say, and often the things needed some work before I could say them the right way—to be understood—and not just shock people or make them turn away. I said it all in one long sentence, like I was running out of breath.

He talked to me then about the difference between journalism, which was writing for newspapers or magazines, and writing imaginative stories or poetry. Which appealed to me most? he wondered. I couldn't tell him about the scads of poems I wrote, all of them bleak and depressing, and showed only to you, dreamy Mr. Allison, who *wandered lonely as a cloud* down the halls.

It was then Mr. Socks came up with a startling idea. "Why don't you phone an accomplished writer? To find out what you should study?"

His idea reminded me a little of the letter Mrs. Antsy had wanted us to write. But in this case, the speaking-to-a-famous-person actually made sense. So I asked, "Which one? Who do I call?"

"Morley Callaghan," he said, like he had his answer ready. "He was in Paris, you know. During the heydays of the 1920s, with Ernest Hemingway and the gang."

I had only a vague notion of this Important Twentieth-Century Writer, and to me he sounded pretty ancient. But I didn't want to be ungrateful. So I tried to look keen when Mr. Socks handed me a slip of paper saying "Morley Callaghan," followed by a phone number.

I still have to laugh out loud at the thought of my phoning the famous writer. At the time I didn't even know how famous, that he'd been nominated for a Nobel Prize. It was around eight o'clock at night, and I was hunched like some spy in my aunt and uncle's bedroom, whispering in the dark. I didn't want them to know what I was doing, in case it didn't work out. I rehearsed what I would say a couple of times, then dialled carefully. I remember how dry my mouth suddenly got.

A man answered, a gruff voice. He seemed surprised and not entirely pleased. "Who? Who's calling?"

I repeated my name. I remember running my fingers over the bed quilt and praying that this was the butler, that Morley himself was not at home. "I'm a student at Emery Collegiate," I murmured.

"A student where?"

"Should I study journalism or English literature?" I stammered.

He sounded as if he was chewing cashews or potato chips,

something crunchy. Then he coughed. Said he was sorry but he was eating dinner. Could I call back later?

I said, sure. And hung up, wondering whether I'd been brushed off for good. Or when the right time might be to call back. I had no idea at what hour writers went to bed, especially famous, grumpy ones. I'd always imagined they stayed up late into the night, drinking wine and getting a hunch, then scribbling frantically.

I almost backed out of phoning him a second time. But I think a certain stubbornness of mind, the thing that earned me all those detentions, helped me out. Plus, I didn't want to report back to Mr. Orange Socks and have him make the call for me. God forbid that should ever happen.

So at ten o'clock, the hour at which decent people went to bed, or so my Aunt Alice often said, I called the number again. And when the same voice answered, I repeated my question. This time he laughed. "Good for you," he said. "I thought maybe I'd scared you off."

"You sounded hungry," I said. I wanted to show sympathy for a writer who was probably too busy to eat. He laughed again, as if he appreciated the thought.

"Here's my advice," he said. "If you seriously want to become a writer, I would read as many books as I could. I would take courses in literature. And then forget half of what you've read and just do what you were going to do in the first place."

I could tell without seeing his face that I was speaking to a man who had mastered most of the uses of irony. And that he hadn't liked some of his school exercises either.

It was a brief conversation, maybe only a minute. And it never occurred to me until recently that you, Bud, Mr. Head-in-the-Clouds Allison, were probably the one behind Mr. Orange Socks coming up with such an inspired idea.

It's strange how I didn't realize that for so long. And how I never thanked you. For so much. For having me read at that poetry festival. Until that night, even my aunt and uncle hadn't heard most of my gloomy verse. You were the only one.

"You're young to be so world-weary," my aunt said, when I was practicing my slowed-down, pausing-for-effect reading voice backstage. In her day poetry was more hopeful, she said. And it rhymed. She gave me a big, long hug that I wanted more of and wanted to break away from, all at the same time. She was right; I was somewhat weary. And more than anything, I was scared.

But you and I both knew, Bud, that the world wasn't perfect. And you made me go on anyway, made me get up in front of all those people and read my poems. I was wearing a velvet miniskirt and black tights, and my voice shook more than once in the echoey sound of the microphone. I couldn't see out into the dark beyond the floodlights. Couldn't see where you were sitting. But afterwards there was applause. It was a kind of recognition for just existing, just being alive. Just being fifteen and being heard.

I should have written you this letter long ago. Before you got so sick with stomach cancer, as though you had something eating you up inside. Maybe it was all that bad cafeteria food at school. Or worrying about your students.

That last time I saw you, do you remember what you said? You admitted you'd turned my first novel face-out on the shelves in that downtown bookstore. You wanted everyone to see it, you said. You were so proud of me. And I think maybe you were relieved that I'd survived, wasn't rocking back and forth, back and forth in some institution like a crazy woman.

I never told you how the whole thing ended with Mrs. Antsy. How I turned that letter into a poem about my mother. I've rewritten it a million times over the years. And have often wished I had given you that one too. The poem so hard to squeeze out of me.

I seem to have developed this habit of writing to the dead. I suppose it's one of the uses of irony.

— Marion

Marion Quednau dedicates this essay to Ann and Lyman Henderson, and yes, to Bud Allison. After a silence of many years, and fearing her old English teacher had died, she has reestablished contact, and they remain good friends.

The Skinny One

Karen Rivers

I am fifteen years old and I am a liar. Let me show you who I am.

Picture this: It is an ordinary suburban kitchen. In the corner is the bird cage, which houses our pet budgie of the moment. The bird—either Eddie, Sammy, Robbie, or Jamie—squawks for attention. On the table is a pile of magazines from which I have cut a picture of a perfect body to stick on the fridge. This is to remind me of what I *don't* look like. The radio is on. I am alone in the house. In the kitchen sink, I pile some dirty dishes. Pots and pans and a glass bowl with ice cream melted in the bottom. I turn the oven on to 375° and leave it there. This is my lie: I have dirtied the dishes, but have not consumed the food.

My parents come home from work and ask, *What did you eat for dinner?*

Chicken, potato, broccoli, carrots, I recite. *Ice cream, cookies.*

My dad says, *I don't know why you can't clean up after yourself.*

My mom says, *Cookies* and *ice cream?*

Here is the funny part. What I *really* ate for dinner was an apple (80 calories). It was a good apple and I was relieved, as it was all I was allowed that day. (This is one of the rules, for alternate days.) If I bite into the apple and find it as dry as sawdust I want to fall to my knees and cry, knowing that the next meal will not come until noon the next day. Other times—the good days—the juice runs down over the red-veined flesh and the apple tastes so sweet that my taste buds ache. This was one of the good days. I ate the whole thing, or at least all of it except the seeds and stem, nibbling away with my pointed teeth, getting every morsel of that sweet flesh onto my tongue. The bird flew to my shoulder to demand his share, but I knocked him off and he fluttered away in a tumult of colored feathers. The apple is all for me. There is none to spare.

After I ate my apple, I was filled with power. I was as light as the bird. I was strong and clean, and most of all I was still hungry. My stomach rang with emptiness. I drank one glass of water and then two. Muted, I went into my room and lay on the rubber-smelling gold carpet. I did a hundred sit-ups, a hundred leg lifts, a hundred push-ups. My muscles protested weakly. *My body is a machine,* I told myself. I forced it to do a hundred more sit-ups. Just a machine.

If my body is *just a machine* then it doesn't matter that I loathe it. Loathe is not even a strong enough word. What I feel is closer to a white-hot anger, a raging hatred. At myself. I have somehow betrayed *me* by growing curves, by spilling rolls of fat over the waistband of my jeans.

Look at me.

In the mirror I see ugly blue-veined breasts that hang like udders, cottage cheese flesh on my ass, stretch marks on my hips from the sudden onset (late) of a much-prayed-for puberty. Puberty doesn't seem to fit or flatter me. I wish I could return it, like an unwanted gift. This is not what I had bargained for, this is not what I meant when I whispered into my pillow, *Please God, give me breasts.* Stupid. Now look at me. Behind the toothpaste flecks and God-knows-what-else on the mirror, there I am. My hair is too short and out of proportion to the width of my body. My posture is terrible. But the flesh—the flesh is what makes my heart pound and my mouth go dry. Too much, too much. I simply take up too much room in the glass.

I stare at myself for a long time, allowing myself to simmer in the acid burn of my self-disgust. My punishment is to stand on the scale. It is green metal and cold under my bare feet. The needle wobbles up to 140, 138 if I rest my hand on the towel rack—142 if I move my left foot. I get off and use the toilet and dry my hair, then weigh myself again, just to see the number fall. After dressing, I do it again to see how much my clothes weigh. I write down the numbers in my diary, beside the graph I have created. I mark a dot next to 138, that being the lowest number of the day, and then I attach that dot to the dot from the previous day. The line is almost flat, but not quite. The graph is my lifeline. On it, I am going to lose ten pounds by Christmas—still two months away. Twenty by the end of the school year. I have already marked the final dot.

This is the plan:

By this summer—the all-important summer between eleventh and twelfth grade—I will weigh 118 pounds. I will have long hair and the right clothes. I will be beautiful and popular, and this popularity will carry me through graduation year in style. I am so swept up in this future fantasy of me that sometimes when I catch a glimpse of my current self, I forget how to breathe. I hyperventilate. How did this happen? *Where did I go?*

What you have to understand is this:

I was always the skinny one. It is my role in this family. I have two sisters. Diane is the oldest one, far enough away in age to be separate, other. She is at university, in a different world. Sonja is the middle one, eighteen months older than me, one grade ahead. She is direct and immediate competition. Here are her roles: *the pretty one, the popular one, the one who gets in trouble.* She is also the fat one. But there is some blurring of that line now, because Sonja is beginning to fade away. She has been on a diet since the seventh grade, but suddenly it is working. She eats rice cakes layered over with peanut butter so thin it is translucent and then she works it off in the gym.

She is the pretty one. But I am the smart one. I am the good one. *I am the skinny one.* If she takes skinny then all I am left with is smart and good, and that is not enough. It smacks too much of nerd, of goody-goody.

I don't put anything on *my* rice cakes at all. Peanut butter is, after all, just flavored fat and oil. I don't need it. I take a rice cake to school for lunch and eat it in front of my locker—fast, before anyone can see me and comment—leaving small pebbly crumbs on the waxed floor. I go to the cafeteria with my friends. *I've already eaten,* I tell them. *I was starving and I couldn't wait.* I buy my diet soda and sip it slowly. I watch them eat. One girl eats an apple fritter every day. She isn't skinny. *Who does she think she is?* An apple fritter! A thousand calories of fat and sugar. I hate her for eating it. I want one so badly my chest aches and my head gets light. The empty sweetness of the diet soda turns over and over in my stomach. I push my chair back so quickly it falls over. I say, *I have to go to the library. I forgot.* I hurry away, head down, heart pounding, my mouth sore from craving so strongly what I am not allowed to have.

Not allowed. Says who? Me. I won't allow it.

In the library, I read books about anorexia. I inspect pictures of the ailing girls: their thin, frail bodies; their bones wrapped tightly with translucent skin; their eyes huge and haunted. They look terrible, they look as though they are dying. I do not look like that, nor will I ever. I certainly don't want to *die.* I will stop at 118 pounds. I read hungrily, hidden in the library carrel. There is useful advice in here, things I need to know. I read about purging—ipecac and laxatives. I promise myself that I will never do that. Not me. I don't have to. I am strong enough to resist the lure of food.

I am the strong one. This is my secret.

The days drag on.

Outside the windows of the school, winter falls like a black curtain. The sky is heavy with low-slung clouds carrying snow and cold and wind. I am in Biology, perched on a wobbly stool at my bench, trying to get fresh air through the window's open crack. The room is pungent with the stench of formaldehyde. On black, rubber-coated pans each one of us has a frog, cut open and held that way with stick pins. The gray organs glisten. The smell is making me thick-headed and fuzzy. It is almost three o'clock. I will soon be crossing the snowy parking lot and getting on a bus for home. I am thinking about what to have for dinner. Today is not an apple day. I am allowed to have something more—maybe a baked potato with a sprinkling of cheese (200 calories) or a small meat pie (240 calories). I am lost in this thought when the teacher approaches. *Well, Karen,* he says. *What do you see?* I stand up and drag my attention back to the grotesquely splayed frog, poking at it with my scalpel. *Um,* I say, gouging at hunks of frog-fat. The fat is almost orange and shaped like Kraft Dinner. Bile rises in my throat.

Fat, I tell him, clenching my teeth.

Very good, he says. *Yes, indeed.*

I sit back down and watch in disgust as my thighs spread flat. I can almost see the horrifying pasta curls of lard through my jeans, my skin. *Fat,* I think. *Fat, fat, fat.* I decide on a new rule. On alternate days, dinner will be a hard-boiled egg (90 calories). No more meat pies or baked potatoes. The rule is formed and set as solid as the ice outside before I have time to think it through, before I have time to change my mind.

It is morning, early. Outside it is still dark. My alarm blares. I need to get up an hour and a half before I leave so that I have a chance against my hair, which always does its own thing regardless. I am cold. The number on the scale is 130, still twelve pounds away from where I need to be. I turn the heat on and stand for a few minutes over the hot-air vent. The room goes bright white and then gray. *I am going to faint,* I realize. I sit down on the toilet and then stand up again. *I'll get help,* I think. Too late. I begin to fall, my head striking first the counter and then the toilet. I hit the floor hard, with a crash that brings my parents running. All around me are the bottles and jars I have inadvertently smashed on the cold tile floor.

I stay home from school. This is good because it means I can get away with eating nothing. All day, I lie on my bed and search for my ribs, carved ivory triumphs so close to the surface of my skin.

I am sixteen years old.

One-eighteen still eludes me. My body is stuck at this weight and won't budge. Worse, I can no longer keep this up. I am too tired and hungry and scared that my constant dizziness will lead to fainting in public. I can't allow that to happen—I am afraid of being noticed, of calling attention to myself. I begin to eat again, first a little, and then more and more. When I close my eyes to sleep, I have nightmares of all that my body is consuming. I can't keep up with my own hunger. I am losing control and I am terrified.

Sonja is well out in front. She takes off her sweater and I can see her ribs curving around to meet her spine. *Bitch,* I think, helplessly.

I break the promise I made to myself and begin to purge. If I hated myself before, now what I feel is so powerful that I find myself shaking all the time. Everything is wrong. Everything. It is Sonja who makes this purging all right: she shows me how to stick my finger down my throat, how to eat and eat and eat and not gain weight. It's okay, she tells me. Everyone does it. Soon our right hands bear the twin marks of bulimia, an open cut on the base of our gagging finger from where it bangs against our teeth. If starving gave me a feeling of control and cleanliness and emptiness, then this brings me the opposite. I take long showers and baths and rinse my hair with vinegar. I brush my teeth until my gums bleed and my teeth gleam, but I cannot rid myself of the stench.

I think: *If people knew I did this, they would hate me.* What people? I don't know, and no longer care. Everything is going to hell. The number on the scale is stuck and I am puffy and tired and have terrible heartburn. The colitis I have been plagued with since childhood is getting worse. Eating too much and then purging provokes bouts of pain so severe that I am left in tears, bent double in bed or running back and forth to the toilet.

I think: *This isn't working. I have to stop.*

I think: *Help.*

And then, my sister is caught. How did it happen? Her tiny body wrapped under all those sweaters.

The truth is, I told on her. I said, *Mom, Sonja has a problem. Just* look *at her. Open your eyes.*

Sonja is taken to an eating disorder clinic and the family caves in a little on itself. The presence of the clinic in our lives is an admission of some kind of failure. Sonja is once again the bad girl. *Karen did it too,* she says, on the defensive. *Ask her.*

Nonsense, says my mother.

My mother blames herself for Sonja's problem. I am helpless with both wanting to tell her about me and wanting her to never know. *She* is not to blame, *she* did nothing wrong. The fact of the matter is that Sonja is sick. Her bony ribs gave her away. My ribs are still well hidden, so I am not sick. I convince myself of this truth.

I go on alone, without Sonja, my partner in crime. I make small deals with God: *Please let me bring up the whole meal, please let me lose weight, please cure me of this weakness and I will never never never do this again.*

Somewhere along the line, and I don't know when it is, I do stop. I stop because I am scared. I am tired of recognizing the red angry marks on other people's fingers, tired of being tired and endlessly dizzy, tired of the burning pain in my chest.

I tried and I failed. I am not used to failing, and somehow this failure in my battle with food and weight fuels me to fail at other things. I have never failed anything before, but now I fail math. I fail to attend classes. I fail to do assignments on time. I fail my driving test. I fail, I fail, I fail. I failed at anorexia. I failed at bulimia. I fail at my attempts at dating. I fail at friendships, which usually collapse under the weight of my insecurities.

It is a few years later that something happens. *Something.*

I am twenty-one.

I have left home, moved away to another city, an apartment of my own. I am trying to reinvent myself once again. My best friend is thin and beautiful and I hate her and I love her. I have known her since I was six years old. When we were kids, she was the fat one. I was the skinny one. She is my new Sonja. Her weight-loss secret involves laxatives. I try it myself but find it aggravates my chronic bowel problem, leaving me weeping and praying on the bathroom floor. I give up quickly, and edge my way back to the more subtle form of starvation condoned by fashion magazines, followed to the letter and punctuated by frantic two-hour daily workouts. I take up running. I am trying to outrun the fat and the fear.

At night, my friend and I go to nightclubs where we sip gin and tonics (dinner) that glow with alien strength under the white lights.

At one of these clubs, I meet a man. Dating changes things. Starvation is no longer an option; it is too difficult a thing to hide. There is less time for working out. I am healthier than I have ever been.

The man's name is Sam. Sam is attractive in a way that makes knees weak. When we go out, other girls stare at him and glower at me. In the washroom, one of them pauses in the application of her lipstick and asks, *What is* he *doing with* you? As if I know. I shrug and try to look as though I don't care what she thinks.

I do care. One day, I am sure he will leave me for a thinner woman.

Sam and I go out to eat. He has friends who own restaurants. We eat huge Italian meals and he makes nebulous promises. *You are real girlfriend material,* he says. *You are someone I could marry.* I collect his words and treasure them, memorize them, tell my best friend what he said.

And then, I get sick.

Suddenly I am unable to keep down the pastas, the cheese-rich pizzas. My stomach aches, dully, constantly. I call home and I say, *Mom, I think there is something wrong with me.*

We talk about it, and when no other obvious answer emerges we decide it is probably just stress.

I do feel stressed, anxious most of the time and vaguely afraid. I sit in my basement apartment with the low ceilings and tiny half-windows and try to eat a piece of toast. It comes up. I sip tea and try to study. Mid-terms are looming and I am behind in my work. Sam does not understand my "sickness." *What do you have to be stressed about?* he asks. I make excuses not to see him. When he calls I tell him, *Not tonight, I have too much to do.*

But I don't go to the doctor. I don't ask for help.

You see, this cloud has a silver lining: I am finally losing weight and I like it. The scale drops down farther and farther.

I am empowered by my new, thinning physique. I break up with Sam. He seems genuinely upset. He says, *I'm going to send my friends over to break your kneecaps.* This is both frightening and funny. I laugh. It seems so unlikely that he would care *that* much. About me? I am not worthy.

I have a low-grade fever that keeps me huddled under blankets, wondering if I should give in and see a doctor. I phone Sonja. *I'm losing weight,* I tell her. I don't know what motivates me to do this. She has recently married and had a baby. She is different now. She seems to have lost her obsession with being thin.

Good for you, she says.

I interpret this as jealousy.

It is Thanksgiving, and I decide to go home. The ferry is delayed due to weather, and I wait in the lineup for three hours. In the warm bubble of my idling car, I paint my nails and listen to the rain drumming on the roof. I want to look good when I get there. I want my family to say, *Karen, you look great, we hardly recognized you.* The exhaust fumes bite into my nose and throat, and I gag. I don't want to be sick. To make my way through the rows of cars to the washroom is too much of a journey.

The ferry arrives. Even in dock, it rocks back and forth like a giant cradle. Passengers crowd up the stairs, but before long people are throwing up in the aisles and clinging, green, to the arms of their chairs. We are like a huge public club of vomiters. I blanch and go back down to the safe sanctuary of my car on the car deck, cold though it is. I curl up under my coat and try to sleep or to hide, or both.

Home is both different and the same. In the kitchen, a budgie named Simon squawks in the corner. Nobody comments on my weight. Nobody says those magic words, *I can't believe how good you look.* Instead they say, *Are you still sick?* I lie and tell them that I'm fine, I'm not sick after all, it must have just been stress.

By dinnertime, for the first time in weeks, I actually *don't* feel sick. I eat first one helping and then another: turkey and potato and carrots and gravy and stuffing. While my sisters feed their kids, I feed myself. The hole inside me is enormous and must be filled. I cram the food in until my belly hurts and I can't eat any more.

After dinner, my sisters vanish downstairs with their children. I don't know where I fit in here. Who am I, now? *The childless one, the sick one, the student, the one who moved away.* Out of habit, I go to the bathroom and weigh myself. One twenty-two. I wonder without really caring if I was at that elusive 118—the magic number—before I ate. I go into my old room and try on clothes from high school. They hang loosely on me. In the mirror, I finally look thin. It is a hollow victory.

Where is my prize? I want it. Now.

In my parents' room, I flop down on the bed and watch TV. My dad is in the kitchen doing dishes, and I can hear the others playing downstairs. I am alone with Barbara Walters or Mike Wallace when suddenly I get dizzy. Very dizzy. I hold still and listen to my body. I turn off the TV. The room swirls and dips. My heart flutters in my chest like a caged bird. Carefully, I get up and walk to the kitchen as though, instead of avocado shag carpet, there is broken glass under my feet.

I say, *Dad, I think I'm going to faint.*

He looks at me and asks, *Why do you always stand up when you think you're going to faint?*

Do I? I wonder idly. *Do I faint often enough for that question to make sense?* Nothing makes sense—not the way the room is moving, not the way a part of me is separating and floating away. I stare at him, at the pile of dirty dishes in front of him in the sink. The budgie has flown onto his glasses and is nuzzling his cheek.

I'm going to lie down, I say. Or I think I do. I don't really know.

This is what happens:

My body falls a great distance, or not at all. I am spiralling away. I am nowhere and everywhere. The sounds of the household give way to silence, and I am warm for the first time in weeks. I open my eyes and look around. I appear to be on a fast-moving train. I am not alone. My family is with me. Outside the train windows, the light is white and blinding. I know, without knowing how, that outside it is deathly cold. The warmth seeps through me. I don't understand what has happened, but I do understand that we have escaped from something unspeakable. On this train, we are finally safe.

I am absolutely not afraid. Being free of fear is a first for me. I am looking at my hands, which are glowing pink in the odd light, marvelling at their heat, when, from a great distance, I hear yelling.

Karen!

Karen!

I think, *Be quiet. Leave me alone.*

I am confused, because the voice is my father's and yet he is here with me on the train, where no one is speaking. He is drawing attention to us, and my sense of safety wobbles.

Am I sleeping? I don't want to wake up. Is this a dream?

Don't make me come back, I think. *Please don't make me.*

Karen!

I open my mouth. I force myself to do it, if only to ask him to stop. I swim up towards him through heavy layers. I try to breathe. It is harder than I thought. Finally, I find my voice.

I say, *What?*

Waiting for the ambulance, I make my mom hold my hand. I clutch on to her and I say, *Don't you dare let me die.*

A sensation of pure terror clings to me like cobwebs. It scares me to realize that I almost didn't come back. I had a choice, somewhere in the depths of the dream: to let the train take me away, or to return to where the voices called. *I don't want to die,* I repeat.

You aren't going to die, my mom says. In my chest, my heart feels enormously heavy. In the distance I hear my dad saying to the ambulance attendant: *I couldn't find her pulse. Her skin was blue.*

In the hospital, I am the lone patient on a soon-to-be-closed ward. Several nurses buzz around me, hooking me up to machines and IVs. I am so tired. I want to sleep but I am afraid that I won't wake up, that I won't want to, that they will let me drift away.

One nurse tells me that I have had a cardiac incident, that my electrolytes are way out of whack. *Have you been sick?* he asks.

Yes, I nod. *I have been sick.*

Days pass. Tests are done, and I am diagnosed with salmonella poisoning. It is an easy answer to accept. *Food poisoning.* The truth is, I have been sick for years, and my sickness has little to do with bacteria, although certainly that is what shifted the delicate balance I created. You would not have looked at me and thought that there was something desperately wrong. I hid my sickness well. I kept my ugly secrets. But now, for the first time, I understand what I have done to myself.

It comes down to this: My body is *not* a machine, after all.

On the day that I am discharged, I weigh 135 pounds.

Going Crazy, Wanna Come?

Susan Musgrave

"I don't advocate drugs, alcohol, violence or insanity—but they've always worked for me."

I began my convocation speech to a high school graduating class several years ago by quoting the journalist Hunter S. Thompson. I said insanity was what had kept *me* sane throughout high school because, among other things, my teeth weren't straight enough for me to be a cheerleader. Most of the graduates I was addressing came from goal-oriented upper-middle-class families. "Forget about goals," I told them. "Sigmund Freud said death is the goal of all life. Sooner or later you'll all reach your goal, so try to live a little in the meantime." The teachers told me afterwards it was the first speech they'd ever seen their students listen to.

The next day twenty outraged parents phoned the principal to complain. I was pleased that, almost thirty years after I had dropped out of high school, I still had the ability to annoy so many parents. I figured I must be doing *something* right.

I've never been the kind of writer who believes she can change the world, but I've always believed it's a writer's job to shake things up, to disturb the status quo. My teachers used to tell me I had the wrong attitude. As far as I'm concerned, it's the only kind of attitude to have. I'm happy to say this particular principal supported me, which is more than my own high school principal had done. When I ended up in his office for necking with my boyfriend instead of paying attention in Biology, "the Monk" (as we called him because of the hair growing out of his ears) told me that if I continued on this downward spiral of kissing boys, writing poetry, and skipping classes, I would most likely end up as a prostitute. But I already knew the world's oldest profession wasn't for me. I didn't want a job where you had to work with other people.

I don't think there is one moment when you realize, This is it, this is who I am, what has just happened to me is going to change my life forever. Instead there are a series of life-altering moments, beginning when you are born and ending when you die, and a great many of these seem to occur in your teenage years.

When you are in the midst of a moment that will change everything, though, it can almost be too bright to see. "I did not know I was living my life then for what I have become," I wrote in a poem called "The Long Way Home." Looking back, it seems as if everything, from the moment I came into the world shaking my fists, until I turned fourteen and dropped acid for the first time, was preparing me for a lifetime of kicking against the pricks.

My rebellion began in the womb. My mother, who claims I was conceived on my father's boat, *Froggy,* during a southeast gale with the ninety-pound storm anchor out, says I stayed up past my bedtime every night and kept her awake with my kicking. It was party time in the womb; I didn't want to waste my nine months sleeping. I was happy there. No one was disappointed in me, there were no expectations except that I would eventually leave. I had everything I needed: food, drink, drugs (my mother had a glass of sherry and a cigarette before dinner every night), four walls, and a roof over my head. Then, at three a.m. on March 12, 1951, I came out of that wet, fleshy darkness into the bright lights, the masked faces of strangers, and that first painful slap. Welcome to your life!

I must have spent the next two years going through withdrawal—certainly there were no more cocktails for me at Happy Hour—because I remember nothing about my babyhood. When I was two my whole family moved to Hawaii: my parents, me, and Charlotte, my security rabbit made from a sock, whose name I pronounced Lalee. I was sick with a mild case of polio on the cruise ship en route, and my mother gave me her china doll, Patsy, to console me as I tossed feverishly in my bunk. Patsy and I were inseparable until the day I dug a grave for her in Waikiki Beach. "I buried Patsy," I told my mother, and then never mentioned her again.

Why did I do this? I have no idea. I still bury things, though: dresses I've worn until the material begins to rot, the boots of Spanish leather with crimson soles and crimson lining that I bought in

Miami, the hair that comes out in my hairbrush. I am constantly burying bits of myself wherever I go.

We returned to my birthplace when I was four. Every night I fell asleep with Lalee. Every night I woke up crying, "I want my Lalee"; by loving her I had worn her out, back into her original sock-shape, and she kept getting tangled in the folds of my nightie with the blue rosebuds on it or in my flannelette sheets. Every night, faithfully, my mother got up, turned on the light, and found my Lalee for me. Finally, though, she got tired of being awakened and threw Lalee into the fire. She wishes now she hadn't, because not only did I keep her awake crying for the rest of the night, I grew up to be a teenager who took drugs. Parents never stop blaming themselves for the mistakes they sometimes make.

Along with Lalee I had a few imaginary friends, like Wind Kite and Maureen Princess Aurora. My parents thought it would be healthier for me to have *real* friends (another mistake) and enrolled me in kindergarten. I ran away the first day, pedalling home on a stolen tricycle. My mother registered me in another kindergarten, much farther away, where the tricycles were kept padlocked in the basement. At naptime the girl lying on the mat next to me tickled me, and when I laughed I was sent to sit on the Thinking Chair in the hall. From then on I tried not to laugh, and pretty soon not smiling at all became a habit. A child psychologist advised my parents to let me drop out of kindergarten.

Grade one looked more promising, until the first day. My teacher was Mrs. Bennett, an older woman who wore sensible shoes and her hair in a bun. I cried and made a scene. I wanted to be in Mrs. Guest's class. Mrs. Guest was younger and dressed with pizzazz: crinolines, hooped skirts, Cinderella-like glass slippers with flowers in their heels. She had been in a Japanese prisoner-of-war camp and had a vaccination mark the size of a mandarin orange on her arm. My mother said it was because they'd used the same needle on everyone.

The following year, when I was assigned to Mrs. Guest's grade two class, I cried and made a scene, because I wanted Mrs. Bennett to be my teacher forever. But Mrs. Guest read us stories each day after lunch, and soon I was transported by the drug of her perfume and the mesmerizing sound of her voice. Every afternoon, just by listening to her read, my mood was altered. (Once it's in your blood, can you *ever* give it up, the desire to alter your consciousness?)

In grade four I fell in a different kind of love with my teacher. Mr. Seale, who was Irish, told me I could end up being a writer one day. For him I wrote horse stories with surprise endings, set in Ireland, epics like "War Glory's Fury." I was sure Mr. Seale had nothing better to do than go home after school and critique my tragedies while his wife peeled the potatoes. He wrote his comments in elegant italic script: "Is this your own work? If so—10/10!"

I was an A student, and an oddball, neither of which enhanced my popularity with my peers. I did earn my classmates' respect briefly in grade seven, when I kicked an apple core at a boy I liked in lineup and had to go and stand in front of the principal's office. But mostly I escaped into writing poetry. One of my first efforts, rhyming couplets about Jackie Kennedy visiting JFK's grave by moonlight, won a prize, a copy of Shakespeare's *Much Ado About Nothing*. Much ado about *nothing?* I wonder now if the judges were trying to tell me not to quit my day job!

"Life, friends, is boring," the great poet John Berryman wrote. I knew what he meant the day I entered high school. The school I attended was for kids from the richest district, per capita, in the country. As well as being from families that were "nouveau riche," as my father said in disdain, the girls who went to my school were beautiful. They had straight, bleached-blonde hair. Their teeth were also perfectly straight, and very white when they smiled, which they did often. They had a lot to smile about. They wore the trendiest clothes and their breasts were several cup sizes bigger than their brains, an asset, as I could plainly see.

I, on the other hand, had untamable hair, a wardrobe courtesy of my granny's church rummage sales, no breasts (yet), and—the bane of my existence—crooked teeth. My parents, of British descent, believed that it would be vain and unpatriotic to have my teeth straightened, and that "fangs" would help build character. So, while the cheerleaders shook their pom-poms, I skulked beneath the bleachers writing countless poems to Count Dracula.

In grade nine I furthered my creative writing skills by forging notes from my parents excusing me from Phys Ed. When my crime was discovered, I was given a detention and sent to sweat it out in the library. The only other time I'd been in this much trouble was when I'd been sent to the Thinking Chair as a kinder-kid for the heinous crime of laughing. It's no wonder I began to equate thinking and books with being "bad," which was now what I had decided to be.

Serving my sentence in the library was a step in my chosen direction. I blew the dust off a few random books of poetry only to discover that they contained everything I'd always wanted to know about sex and violence but had not been able to ascertain from my Guidance counsellor or my selected readings from Henry Miller's hot trilogy, *The Rosy Crucifixion.* Not only were these subversive modern poets writing about a taboo subject, they did so without using rhyme and meter, and they used four-letter words to express their carnal feelings. I wasn't experienced enough to write about sex very deeply, but my love affair with modern poetry led me to become more experimental. I wrote poems full of words I didn't understand, such as "Evolutionary Obsequies."

Around the same time I discovered Bob Dylan. Real life, I got the message from his lyrics, had less to do with wandering lonely o'er Wordsworthian hills of daffodils than it had to do with ghettos and human rights demonstrations, smokestacks and factories. I had experienced none of these in the prosperous west-coast city where I lived. But I had an imagination. I wrote free verse set in Chicago about cigarette butts drowned in cups of cold coffee. To gain worldly experience, I took off from school and ran away from home with my boyfriend. For a day, until the police picked us up and drove us back to our parents, I sat moodily on the railway tracks writing my "Ode to Existence" and "Ode to Futility." Through the process of writing poetry, I learned that life felt a lot less futile after you had finished writing about it.

I learned one other thing, too: writing paid off because writing could *pay*. As I advanced through school I turned my talent for forging notes into a profitable business by excusing my fellow students (on their parents' behalf) from almost every subject. Grade ten was one of the most prolific and lucrative periods of my writing life.

In 1967, the year I dropped out of high school for good, I was assigned an essay on the topic of "Where I Am Going on my Summer Vacation." Most of my classmates were honest enough to write "nowhere," but I said I was going crazy. It turned out to be foreshadowing.

That spring I'd had my first hit of LSD laid on me (as we used to say) by my boyfriend, the son of a math professor at the local university. The tab of Orange Barrel was a Valentine's Day present my boyfriend had had laid on *him* by Crowbait, a self-ordained priest who had meditated transcendentally and travelled through India sleeping in ditches on purpose.

Crowbait's worldliness astounded me. He promised us we could fly higher than the Milky Way on TransLove Airways if we swallowed that blotter of acid with him in the eye of the cement octopus at a nearby playground. Coming down at five o'clock the next morning, we all climbed an oak tree under a tangerine sky and shared a box of Cocoa Puffs.

For the next six months, I experimented. I was still not, as Jimi Hendrix would have said, "experienced." In fact, I was pretty innocent.

Even though I could spell "Evolutionary Obsequies," I had never smoked a cigarette, inhaled marijuana, or taken a drink of anything stronger than eggnog at my parents' annual Boxing Day party. But now I went with my boyfriend and Crowbait to our friend Christina's studio in the ritzy district every Friday night and dropped acid: Black Double Dome, Purple Haze, Blue Cheer, Yellow Sandoz, Gray Barrel. Christina was an artist from Santa Barbara whose parents were millionaires. She went to a private girls' school and owned everything from a Rolls-Royce to her own armadillo skull. When we were high she would place the armadillo skull on her head and we would stare into her mirror, watching our bodies metamorphose from babies into adolescents into old people, and finally into skeletons.

I began writing Cocoa Puff–induced poetry in that Summer of Love, when, as Grace Slick and Jefferson Airplane sang, one pill made you larger and one pill made you small. The living was easy. All we had to do was reject our middle-class backgrounds, run away from home with beads around our necks and bells on our toes, and smoke the fat reefers laid on us by Crowbait to help us have a trippier time on our way to San Francisco. In Haight-Ashbury we learned how to wear a peace button the right way up and to believe in the slogan, *If it's fun I'll play but not if it's a game.* We fed our heads with acid, grass, and speed, ate brown rice, and advocated free love, not war (though even at sixteen I was streetwise enough to know love always came with a price tag). When the flowers died in my hair and my peace button got stolen, I hitchhiked home. I started coming down the moment I hit the city limits.

I suppose it was a combination of things—not just the drugs—that sped me through the Summer of Love and into a mental hospital. The truth was, so much peace and love had driven me crazy, so far crazy that I even told the two police officers who picked me, bleeding from the wrists, off my parents' bathroom floor that they were beautiful people. My deep thoughts were wasted on them. They seemed more concerned about not getting blood on the interior of their new cruiser, and they confiscated my beads so I couldn't try to hang myself on my way to the psych ward.

At the hospital (which the inmates had nicknamed "the Garden of Eden" because everyone who was committed fell in love, usually with someone else's lover), I met most of the local university's English Department, and a few kids my own age who had literally blown their minds on drugs. But fate has always been kind to me. My psychiatrist knew Robin Skelton, an established poet who taught creative writing and edited a literary magazine. He told Robin about "the young girl in the hospital writing poetry," and Robin came to visit me. Over tea in the cafeteria, Robin asked to see some of my writing, and I showed him my notebooks. He looked up at me after he finished my poem "Going Crazy, Wanna Come?"

"You are not mad," he said. "You're a poet."

Writing those words today, all these years later, I start to cry.

Robin took away some of my poems and published them. I bought my first typewriter with the $100 cheque. He also left me a copy of Sylvia Plath's book of poems, *Ariel,* and Allen Ginsberg's *Howl.* Ginsberg wrote, "I saw the best minds of my generation destroyed by madness." Plath said, "The blood jet is poetry. There is no stopping it." Poetry had given me my life back.

I spent most of my days in the Garden of Eden holed up in my room, writing and reading poetry. I had never been able to write anything while I was high—and not much when I was coming down, because I got too depressed—but now that I wasn't dropping acid I had to do *something* with my mind. I had overfed my head, and it was time to make sense of what I'd ingested.

The first time I ventured from the safety of my room to try socializing in the hospital's common room (which I was required to do to show I was getting well), I met a 250-pound English professor from Berkeley who had been committed for writing FUCK and WAR on the blackboard and asking his students which was the dirty word. He loaned me a book called *The Poet's Calling.* He and I dropped Thorazine and other medications we had saved up until we had enough to get high. We also fell in love.

Love was in the air, all right; even my psychiatrist succumbed to it. He tried to seduce me in his office, first by inflicting on me his unmarketable verse—"My wiry body oozes with goose-bumpy joy. Sex is like swallowing shards of glass, the pain a constant reminder that you are not empty"—then by trying to force his tongue down my throat. When I wouldn't unlock my crooked teeth, he began to cry and said he wasn't cut out for psychiatry. Shortly afterwards the English professor and I escaped from the hospital through an unlocked door marked *Emergency Exit— Admissions Only*. We drove his psychedelic VW van all the way back to California. I continued to write, still focusing on death as a viable alternative but making no further attempts at killing myself. By the Fall of Love, even trying seemed pointless. As the poet Charles Bukowski wrote, "Suicide fails as you get older. There's less and less to kill." I was an authority on aging by then. I was about to turn seventeen.

In 1997, those of us who had survived the intervening years met for a reunion in Christina's attic. There I discovered four lines of poetry written in pencil on her studio door. They had a familiar ring. Crowbait, now a successful realtor who goes by his given name, Harold, said to me, "You wrote that. Trippy, eh? The summer you freaked out on us. Don't you remember?"

They say if you remember the sixties you weren't really there. Whether or not I remembered, I must have been there, for here was evidence, in these immortal lines.

> Is there in this field of gypsies
> And the emptiness of their wandering songs
> Is there a favoured child of beauty
> Bruised and irremediably bereft?

I detect a smattering of Plath in the "bruised" part, but "irremediably bereft"? Trippy, eh? All these years later I still don't know what it means.

About the Authors

Carellin Brooks is a writer and editor. She recently co-edited *Carnal Nation: Brave New Sex Fictions,* and she is also the editor of *Bad Jobs: My Last Shift at Albert Wong's Pagoda and Other Ugly Tales of the Workplace.* To anyone struggling through a hellish teenagehood, she says, "Keep living. It does get better."

Melanie Little's fiction and non-fiction have been published in numerous periodicals, and she has been a contributor to Scribner's Best of the Fiction Workshops. She is working on a full-length memoir about her experiences as a figure skater.

Susan Musgrave has been nominated, and has received awards, in four different categories of writing. Her most recent collection of poetry is *What the Small Day Cannot Hold: Collected Poems 1970–1985,* and her third novel, *Cargo of Orchids,* was published in the fall of 2000. She no longer does LSD, but has never stopped running away.

MK Quednau won a national first-novel award for *The Butterfly Chair* in 1988. She also writes poetry and short fiction. In her teaching and editorial work she has often assisted writers for young readers, and she is secretly working on a young adult novel, knowing that secrets carry us to and from childhood.

Karen Rivers is the author of *The Tree Tattoo, Dream Water,* and *Waiting to Dive. Surviving Sam* is her latest novel. She is frequently overwhelmed by the mass of future writing in her head that has yet to make it onto a piece of paper.

Madeleine Thien has had fiction published in literary magazines and collections, including *The Journey Prize Anthology.* She has also written and recorded for radio. Her first book of short stories, *Simple Recipes,* was published in 2001.

Marnie Woodrow published her first book of short stories at the age of twenty-two, her second collection at age twenty-six. Since then she has been busy getting older and making lots of interesting mistakes. Her first novel will be published in spring 2002. She can be reached via her website at www.marniewoodrow.com.